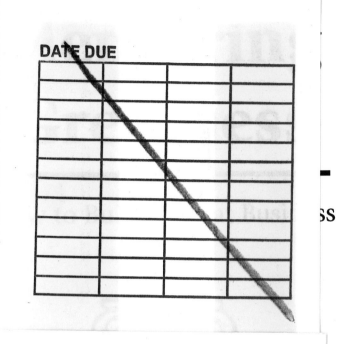

Mentoring
Greatness

How to Build a Great Business

Harold E. Johnson

Director of Operations: Robin L. Howland
Project Manager: Bryan K. Howland
Editor: Word Association
Book and Cover Design: FirstPublish

10 9 8 7 6 5 4 3 2 1

ISBN 1-58000-101-7

Griffin
PUBLISHING GROUP

2908 Oregon Court, Suite I-5
Torrance, CA 90503
Phone: 310.381.0485
Fax: 310.381.0499

Manufactured in the United States of America
Printed by QUESTprint.

To my grandchildren, Rachel and Kyle,
the consummate knowledge workers.
May your joy of learning always be fresh.

Contents

Foreword

In my career as a developer and manager of health care products businesses, my primary responsibility is to provide and create the environment in which good people can grow great companies. Two of these businesses, Cooper Laboratories, Inc. and CooperVison, Inc., grew to become "Fortune 500" companies. From the rigorous strategic planning process we followed, I developed a skill in organizational development—often a somewhat two dimensional discipline in the way it is practiced. If mentoring was part of my practice of the skill, it was more likely coincidental than incidental.

What Hal Johnson has done in his business career, and so brilliantly in his many lectures, books, and articles, is to add the third dimension of mentoring to the practice of organizational development and management. Mentoring and the "caring" implicit in it, enrich the mind, body, and spirit of both the mentor and mentee beyond the knowledge gained and the experiences shared. I wish we had had access to Hal's teaching and preaching on mentoring in the early days of my career. We would have applied its lessons to achieve even greater successes for our businesses and to bring great joy to the lives of our fellow workers. That is why I am writing this brief foreword for Hal. I believe he spells out succinctly in the following pages the steps necessary to build a great company by helping good people to grow. In particular, I appreciate the emphasis on these three vital points:

> Build the strongest team you can and keep developing it.
> Find the best people, build great relationships, and keep looking for what else you can do to create greatness.

Never stop learning. Knowledge makes the difference. Smart people want to   keep building their knowledge base—and use it to create greatness.

Develop leadership at all levels. Leadership with courage to always follow your convictions is what creates greatness.

Those seeking to develop greatness in their businesses will do well to heed the experienced counsel offered in this book. Enjoy!

Parker Gilbert Montgomery
Founder and former CEO
Cooper Laboratories, Inc. and
CooperVision, Inc.

Acknowledgments

When someone finishes a major project, there usually is a host of people who have made important contributions. Such is the case here. Writing my second book was going to be easier—I thought. It was still a lot of work. There has been some wonderful assistance provided that moved the project from my several notebooks of ideas to what you hold in your hands.

I offer a very special thanks to my colleagues at LeadershipONE— Kurt Glassman, Linda Williams, Steve Sevran, Mike Santiago, Susan Glassman, Dan Wilson, Paul Gallagher, and John Olsen. Your support and feedback have been invaluable. It could not have happened without you. You are a wonderful team of colleagues with whom I am honored to be associated.

To my friends at Griffin Publishing I say a special hearty thanks; Bob, Robin, Mark, and Bryan—we made it!

Business colleagues with whom I connect, meet or chat every once in a while—over the months, and years—as well as being readers, you have contributed more than you know—Gary McDonald, Jim Matthew, Clarke Ashton, John Hansen, Cam Carlson, Ed Sultan, Ashley Montague, Larry Prater, Dan Fast, Neil Goldschmidt, Vernon Woo, Kevin Sorensen, Tim Guard, Charles Lau, Mike Roley, Chuck Woods, Steve Dunn, Tamiko Ishidate, Tom Jones, Boyd Baugh, Ken Baugh, Parker Montgomery, Brad Johnson and Gary Black. To you all, thank you from my heart.

I am especially indebted to my fellow authors who have kindly offered their views and insights: Chuck Kremer, Dick Buxton, Ron Martin, and Jim Horan. You were terrific. In spite of your extremely busy schedules, you took the time to offer meaningful feed-back and guidance. Thank you.

Certainly not last—really first—is my family, headed by my incredible wife, Adeline. You make it all doable and worthwhile. I am grateful for you all. And, thank you for your contributions to and support for this project.

To you all I say the most heartfelt thank you. I am deeply indebted for your contributions at so many levels.

Introduction

CEOs and Their Leadership Teams

This is not the easiest time in business to achieve successful results. Business has never been easy, but as this material goes to press, all business leaders are focused on what they can do to improve the odds of predictable success. Business is no longer a game for amateurs. Business is a game where "survival of the fittest" truly applies.

My career has been an exciting one of being a "transition" CEO. I have specialized in the role of instituting rapid change to get a business on track. I should add that I specialize in small-to-medium size businesses (under $250 million). My first task has always been to assess my executive team, make changes where necessary, then get to work mentoring them on basic business blocking and tackling and the game plan. I am particularly gratified to read Jim Collins's research, covered in his new book, *Good to Great*, regarding the priority of having the right team of players. He identifies that the first priority of the CEOs of great companies was to make sure they had the right team even *before* the business direction was complete. Collins found that the CEOs of great companies understood that success was based not so much on markets, technology, competition, or products. While these are very important, the defining advantage is the quality of the management team. The quality and preparedness of the management team will have the greatest impact on your ability to achieve and maintain positive business results. The CEO's job is to create the best possible team.

My experience in assessing executive teams and developing mentoring programs for CEOs and their teams has been an eye opener. I am astonished at what a low level of effectiveness so many executive teams achieve and accept. Even when very talented people are involved, I am finding significant lapses in clarity in how to achieve and maintain high levels of effectiveness. A huge opportunity exists in the business environment to increase the impact of the executive team on overall business results.

Greatness

The title of this book, *Mentoring Greatness,* is the result of a conversation with one of my clients. I asked him what he wanted for his business; he said, "greatness." That opened up a dialogue about what it took for a company to become "great" that aligned with business mentoring. In particular, we discussed how his executive group could be prepared to assist him in the quest for greatness— specifics that were currently not in their execution lexicon. I have concluded that the difference between being a good company and being a great company is based more on *clarity* than anything else. By clarity I mean understanding what is vital and what is not. However, clarity is greatly dependent on knowledge. Building the right knowledge is essential for clarity. The best delivery system for critical business knowledge is mentoring.

The Case For Mentoring

In late 1997 my book *Mentoring for Exceptional Performance* was published. The material for that book was developed over a number of years based on experiences during my career, which has been heavily involved in mentoring. I define "mentoring" as facilitating, guiding, and encouraging continuous innovation, learning, and growth. Essentially this is the key to successful business perpetuation. In that book I described the various approaches to mentoring with the fundamental recommendation that CEOs consider the power of a mentoring program that reaches the individual, the team, and the business culture.

Mentoring is not a "flavor of the month", or flash in the management pan. The concept is centuries old. The first account of mentoring is found in the book of Proverbs in the Old Testament, which, according to biblical scholars, dates back to the tenth century B.C. Here the term "counselor" is used, describing the same process of a mentor. It parallels the use of the term "mentor" which is first seen in Homer's *Odyssey*, written between 800 and 900 B.C. Mentoring has been around a while.

Putting Mentoring to Work

Too few people in business have had the benefit of a mentor. There are some meaningful exceptions, but that is what they are—exceptions. The material I have prepared identifies the benefits of implementing a broad-based mentoring program in your business and describes how to build a great company. My first book focused more on the why of mentoring with general materials to address in building a mentoring program. This book addresses *how* you do it and *how* to get started. Even more to the point, I have included material in Part I, "What Mentoring Can Do for You", that describes how mentoring helps build "greatness" as well as the value of your business.

Part II, "What to Mentor", provides "content focus"—the critical subject matter for business mentoring. In other words, mentoring is a productive activity, but to make it more so, a strategic process of mentoring performance while building knowledge creates enormous returns—perhaps even greatness.

Content Focus—What to Mentor

I have prepared for your consideration a "how and what to mentor" approach to topics that I believe are crucial for excellence in business performance. The mentoring material is focused on what I call the Six Disciplines of Championship Performance. Then within each of these performance areas I describe the *best business practices* I have seen applied to achieve great business results. These practices may not comprise the ultimate list of best practices, but I'm willing to bet the ones presented in the following material, applied diligently, will produce great results.

To bring to life real examples of mentoring intervention, I have included some stories from my client files as well as some of my own CEO experiences. I have changed the identities for purposes of anonymity, except for the one business I would like to highlight that is creating greatness. Pivot Interiors, Inc., in San Jose, California, one of the largest Herman Miller dealers, receives special recognition in the last chapter. Boyd Baugh, chairman of Pivot, shares some of the insights and history of his team's development and guidance principles that have created a great company.

In addition, at the end of each chapter I have included a list of several books around which a discussion group could be organized. I include a description in the material on how these "knowledge development for common usage" meetings can be both productive and fun. Leadership in achieving clarity in business direction and execution is based on the growth of business knowledge. This book shows you the steps. The CEO needs to lead the charge.

How to Use This Book

I have written this book to assist business leaders in developing their intellectual capital. What your troops know and how they use it will make a difference in the future of your business. And yes, an initiative to improve your intellectual capital will take leadership with resolve. If this were easy, everybody would be doing it. Is winning a championship event easy? Of course not—winning awaits those who have diligently prepared and execute well. The same is true with business greatness. To get your business ready to play the game at the highest level, here's what I suggest:

1. Get familiar with the concepts and practices presented in this book.
2. Have your management team read it.
3. Have an off-site meeting to evaluate "what else we can do!" to build greatness in your business. Determine if you can incorporate mentoring. If so, continue.
4. Conduct a team workshop around Part I—"What Mentoring Can Do for You."
5. Jointly evaluate your business performance using the Six Areas of Championship Performance (see

Performance Capability Questions and Characteristics of Businesses at Risk, chapter 4)

6. Draw conclusions about your opportunities.
7. Conduct a team workshop around Part II—"How to Put Mentoring to Work."
8. Develop your strategy for greatness.
9. Get buy-in.
10. Go to work.

Challenge

In the following material you will learn that to achieve great results you need to be continuously asking yourselves, "What else can I do?" The answer often is related to acquiring new performance-enhancing knowledge. That is foundational for continuous improvement. The acquisition of the right knowledge is the starting point for building great performance. Mentoring is the most effective and efficient delivery-change process. My hope is that you will find this book will enrich your process of achieving great business results.

Hal Johnson
San Francisco

Part I

What Mentoring Can Do for You

Chapter 1
Seeking Greatness

"If people knew how hard I had to work to gain my mastery, it wouldn't seem wonderful at all."
—Michelangelo

- Reinventing the Business
- Creative Destruction
- The Role of Knowledge
- Law of Diminishing Expertise
- Leading Knowledge Workers
- Commitment to Learning

Reinventing the Business

One of my clients, when asked what his goal was for his company, responded, "Greatness." Making money was certainly of interest, but he was equally concerned about achieving a position in his business segment that would warrant an evaluation by his peers and colleagues, relative to the business results created, that his company was "great," it did great things, it achieved great results. His particular business is engineering and architecture. His product is right out there for everybody to see—and evaluate.

We spent some interesting time together considering what creates greatness in a business, describing what it looks like, and developing steps to put his business on the path to greatness.

What creates greatness in a company? What enables a particular business to continue to be successful year after year, even with top leadership changes? First of all, it is not just one or two things. Many elements contribute to the process. One of the most essential elements, however, must be the ability to embrace the new while at the same time dealing with the old. Essentially that involves re-inventing the business while staying the course. How does a company do that? This goal is achieved by vigorous, energized people —a company's most valuable asset who can tend to today's business while looking for better ways to capture tomorrow.

Creative Destruction

The business world is currently abuzz concerning the retirement of the most successful CEO of the twentieth century—Jack Welch at GE. To put Welch's accomplishments in perspective, an article in the *Wall Street Journal* related that during the twenty years Welch was at the helm, GE outperformed the S&P 500 by a significant margin—every year. Over this twenty-year period, from 1981 to 2001, the S&P 500 averaged an annual increase in value of 14.3 percent, while GE averaged 21.3 percent—which is almost 50 percent better!

How did Welch do it? No simple answer emerges, but at the core was a burning commitment to eliminate an internal business unit when its rate of change was less than the rate of market change. This process was termed "creative destruction" shedding the old while building the new. The marvel is doing it in a company that has achieved a $400 billion market capitalization. Welch has also said many times that the great achievements of GE were based in the commitment to "raise the intellectual level of the organization by taking everyone's ideas, constantly searching the world for the best ideas and making sure everyone knows their ideas count." What is the lesson for the rest of us in smaller business environments? The lesson is: we had better work as smart as we possibly can. The success driver of the future is knowledge.

The Role of Knowledge

While many of us have been working in the marketplace over the past twenty to thirty years, a very significant change has occurred in the work environment. Essentially we have seen the work environment evolve from one of mostly manual work and worker to one of knowledge work and worker. The most valuable assets of a twentieth century company were its production equipment. Management was focused on increasing the productivity of the manual workers in manufacturing. But the most valuable assets of the twenty-first century enterprise are knowledge workers and their productivity. "Knowledge worker," is a term management guru Peter Drucker coined some thirty years ago. Knowledge workers essentially contribute what they do based on what they know. Knowledge is the driver. But many managers have not found an effective strategy to address this change, if they have even thought about it at all. The development of knowledge has not yet become a key strategy in most businesses.

The knowledge base of a twenty-first century company walks out the door every evening. Do you think employees affect business if they

1. Are not mobilized or unified to create the best out comes?
2. Don't feel like their company really appreciates them or recognizes their contribution?
3. Believe the company doesn't help them understand specifically what knowledge they are responsible to attain, contribute, and maintain?

Leading an enterprise comprised mostly of knowledge workers has its own set of requirements to be successful. Today's manager-leaders have to acquire vast amounts of new knowledge in meeting their responsibilities.

"FRED FEELS OBSOLETE. HIS 9 YEAR OLD GRANDSON JUST DOWNLOADED 50 PAGES OF RESEARCH OFF THE INTERNET, AND FRED FORGOT HOW TO OPEN 'WORD.'"

Law of Diminishing Expertise

Recently an article appeared in *Inc.* magazine that struck a chord. Marketing specialist Martin Jacknis observed a trend in hiring that should be worrisome to business leaders. It should be worrisome to the point of taking a hard look in your organization to see if it is happening and if it is, confronting it immediately.

Simply stated, the Law of Diminishing Expertise holds that leaders tend to hire people whose ability and expertise are beneath their own. That is followed by the next level of managers who also hire people with ability and expertise below theirs. As a result, as the organization grows and more people are hired, the number of people with low expertise far exceeds the number of leaders who possess much greater expertise. It is also true that undeveloped people hire less developed people. The result of this phenomenon is a rapid decrease in performance capability. The off-set is to improve the hiring source as well as the process. Hire the most highly developed leaders you can. Then get your leadership involved in developing those around them. Build, build, build—that's what the great companies do.

Leading Knowledge Workers

As predicted by Peter Drucker some thirty years ago in his book *The Age of Discontinuity*, we now find ourselves in the age of the "knowledge worker." The daunting responsibility now placed on the business leader in the beginning of the 21st century is how to lead knowledge workers effectively. Think about it. Your job as a business leader is to help your colleagues contribute to the enterprise's productivity by using the particular knowledge that they bring to the enterprise. Have you ever thought about the quality of the knowledge you are relying on to get the job done for which you have responsibility? One of the goals of this material is to cause you as a knowledge leader to consider these questions:

1. What specific knowledge do my colleagues require to perform effectively?

2. Where are they currently in their knowledge asset base?

3. How effectively are they prepared to deploy that knowledge?

4. What must I do to help with the development and use of the knowledge?

5. What are the most effective ways to keep knowledge growing and to apply it effectively?

The essence of leadership is performance. Would performance be more likely to improve if greater attention is focused on the quality of the knowledge under your leadership? While this may seem like a "no brainer" question, I don't see a lot of knowledge-building strategies in play in the small-to medium-sized businesses I work with. In fact, I believe the broad use of mentoring to build intellectual capital in any organization is extremely rare. Enormous opportunity exists to do so.

On an intellectual level many businesspeople agree that these are important issues. However, the businessperson often falls back into the same old comfortable rut until his or her comfortable world faces a crisis. Then recovery is usually slow and painful. I firmly believe our business leaders need to stop and consider just what it will take to acquire and maintain effective knowledge worker productivity. Consider these seven major factors that impact knowledge worker productivity.

Seven Major Factors That Impact Knowledge Worker Productivity

1. Clarity of Task
It is essential to ask the question, "What is the task?" This helps add clarity to what knowledge is required.

2. Self-Management
All knowledge workers must be responsible for their own productivity. They have to manage themselves.

3. Continuing Innovation
Continuing innovation has to be a part of the work and the responsibility of knowledge workers. They need to be looking for better ways.

4. Continuous Learning
Knowledge work requires continuous learning and teaching by knowledge workers. Both intake and output are essential.

5. Quality and Quantity Output
Both quality and quantity are important in the productivity of knowledge workers.

6. Recognition of Intellectual Capital
Knowledge workers need to be recognized as an "asset." They represent intellectual capital to the enterprise.

7. Positive Attitude

The attitude of knowledge workers is important to productivity; they must want to work for the enterprise instead of for others.

Commitment to Learning

I have always considered myself a teaching CEO. Where have I found the material to teach? The management leaders who have gone before us and those whose wisdom enabled exceptional performance, provide enormous resources. And then I have endeavored to expand and enrich these resources with real-life experiences.

For over thirty years I have been involved in leading some form of business transition. I have served as the CEO of eight very different businesses, taking them through various "change experiences." In addition, I have had the opportunity and privilege to serve on numerous boards of directors. I have faced lay-offs, cutbacks, explosive growth, great prosperity, stagnation, and most recently, the "new economy" shake out. And yes, I have my share of scar tissue. Few make it through the demands of business processes unscathed. So what I am about to share with you is not a lot of theory. This really works. And like the old economy, which didn't really go away, real success takes a lot of hard work. But working smart can make the hard work more productive. Leading and mentoring knowledge workers to become motivated about their contribution is essential to building a great company. That is the essence of the material to follow.

For Further Reading—Mentoring Material

James Collins and Jerry Porter. *Built to Last—Successful Habits of Visionary Companies* (New York: HarperBusiness, 1994).

Peter F. Drucker. *Management Challenges for the 21st Century* (New York: HarperBusiness, 1999).

Michael E. Porter. *Competitive Advantage—Creating and Sustaining Superior Performance* (New York: Macmillan, 1985).

Chapter 2
Building Greatness In Your Business

"It is not the strongest of the species that survive, nor the most intelligent, but the one most responsive to change."
—Charles Darwin

- Building Greatness:
  What Does It Look Like?
- Business Overview
- Just-In-Time Knowledge
- The Right Knowledge
- Championship Performance—
  Best Business Practices
  Development
- Preparation
- Building Greatness—
  The Right Culture

Building Greatness: What Does It Look Like?

For the past couple of decades, I have been a student of the kind of companies that seem to continually post excellent performance. How do they do that? While each case has its own "flavor," there definitely are some very significant commonalities.

One of the all-time best-selling business books is *Built to Last*. Published in 1994, it continues to be a popular reference on what successful companies have done to perpetuate greatness. The authors, James Collins and Jerry Porras, call these companies "visionary" because they had the vision to see and understand what it took to perpetuate a very high level of performance—and do it. Here's the criteria the authors used to define "visionary,"or what I call "greatness:"

- Established as a premiere institution in its industry
- Widely admired by knowledgeable businesspeople
- Made an indelible imprint, made their mark
- Had multiple generations of chief executives
- Been through multiple life cycles

What were the practices of these great companies? What was it specifically that contributed to their protracted success? While leadership undeniably was a significant element, I contend that is a constant. Let's go one step further. What was it the enlightened leadership decided to stress in their leadership roles? Generally the commonalities of the great companies can be summarized in the following attitudes or mottoes:

1. Commitment to be the best.
2. The company itself is the ultimate creation—not the product.
3. More than profits (not at any cost).
4. Preserve the core/stimulate business.
5. BHAGS—Big Hairy Audacious Goals.
6. Powerful cultures.
7. Try a variety of approaches and keep what works.
8. Home-grown management.
9. Good enough never is.
10. The journey is endless.

Business Overview

To compete in today's market, companies must continually develop their business knowledge in time to have an impact on the business. The new market is the old market; the best practices are still the most effective. Executive teams that fully utilize the best business practices succeed in a hyper-change environment. There is a need to make certain their current business knowledge is based on the best business practices.

Just-in-Time Knowledge

We consistently hear and read that change is occurring in business at an accelerating rate. In his book, *Business @ The Speed of Thought*, Bill Gates observes that there will be more change in the next ten years than there was in the past fifty years. The BIG impact in the business environment is in knowledge. We now live in the era of the knowledge worker. Yet I am astounded at the consistent lack of a knowledge development strategy in businesses. Here we have the most significant contributor to a company's valuation and its competitiveness—what it knows and how well it uses what it knows—yet in most companies, it remains un-addressed strategically. An incredible opportunity exists!

Consider that the most common cause of business failure is the business outgrowing its people. Successful business perpetuation is human resource dependent. A business prepared to meet the increasing demands of change must ask "Are we adequately preparing our people for the future?" and respond accordingly.

Most businesses are impacted by "unconscious incompetence." It's what they don't know that they don't know that usually does the damage. By using the practices described in this material, however, you'll find out what you may or may not know about what kind of team player and leader you are and what you can do about unconscious incompetence. Addressing high-performance growth needs will prepare your company to compete more effectively in an increasingly demanding, competitive environment.

Preparing for change starts at the top. Companies that have managed change and experienced long-term success generally have an executive team committed to lifelong learning, while modeling and mentoring personal growth and development to their associates. That's how change is successfully managed and how it becomes part of the company culture. The key to successfully perpetuating a business is to create a work force committed to creatively anticipating and meeting tomorrow's demands with confidence. How do you achieve this result? Following sound, proven, performance-enhancing principles is the key.

The Right Knowledge

The developmental material presented in this book is aimed at assisting emerging companies to manage their businesses effectively in a hyper-change environment. Many businesses have been started by brilliant, technically oriented entrepreneurs who grew the business to the point that the management requirements became quite daunting. Critical knowledge of the basic processes involved in successfully running a company is also needed.

Best practices is a concept most often associated with manufacturing. However, it also has shown great success in communicating standards of performance in management matters. It is not unreasonable to conclude that through various applications of wisdom, theory and trial and error, that some ways to achieve desired outcomes are more effective than others. I have studied successful organizations and the not-so-successful organizations during this past decade. A definite pattern emerges in the management and leadership behaviors of companies that attain success year after year. It is also true for those that lose their momentum. Consider the following summary.

Patterns of Business Behaviors

Patterns of Success
- Visionary cultures
- People development
- Integrated strategic planning and implementation processes
- Outstanding performance—best business practices

Patterns of failure
- Business outgrows the people
- Entrepreneur fails to transition
- Risk averse
- Vision, strategy disconnected from implementation

The difference in levels of performance is a reflection of the quality of the leadership. The business that consistently posts positive results is lead by a team of successful manager-leaders. Leaders want to answer the question: "What else can I do?" Leaders want to know what they need to know, realizing that they may not know something critical. They want to get it right. They are looking for the best business practices. They attend professional management seminars and tech groups. They invest in training and development to raise the knowledge bar in their organization. They recruit great people and work to help them become even greater. They know how to execute and they are driven for success.

On the other hand, it's hard to understand how some businesses get into trouble when they basically have viable businesses. There are numerous contributors, but those summarized above are most representative. Please remember, I'm addressing businesses in the mostly small-to-medium sector—under $250 million in annual revenue. The primary contributor for business failure is not doing the right things on a timely basis—unconscious incompetence. Leaders did not access the right knowledge on a timely basis, and the business outgrew the management.

Here's a brief glimpse of one of my early experiences with a business having exceptional growth that exceeded the ability of management to respond effectively.

I was nearing completion of a major project in Seattle when an attorney friend of mine called regarding a client of his who was experiencing difficulties with his business. The client had a fast-growing cable television company in the Southwest that served about fourteen cities. The rapid growth was driving extensive capital development—stringing cable—which had created a financial crisis.

It was a classic case of too much growth for a group of under-prepared managers. (To maintain anonymity, I have changed the location and some identifying elements, but the data is factual.) Initially, I worked with the entrepreneur-majority shareholder (let's call him Fred) on an advisory basis while I completed other assignments. After about four months, he asked me to accept the CEO position.

Here are a few "wonderments" I discovered:

1. Instead of paying the program suppliers, funds that should have been allocated to keeping current on programming expense went to capital improvements. In other words, the suppliers were the source of funding for capital development. They had not been invited into this creative financing program and the more significant ones (with invoices totaling a minimum of seven figures) were threatening legal action.

2. Fred was an easygoing, uncomplicated guy. He started his career by installing a community television antennae in his foothill neighborhood and selling subscriptions when he was in high school. He grew up with cable television technology.

3. Fred had a winning personality that created an immediate positive connection. He had good people skills and was very earnest and hard working. However, he had no managerial training and had built his company with others of similar backgrounds.

4. Cable television franchises were awarded by the local municipalities. Once awarded there was no competition. As long as the service was provided, the franchises continued to be renewed.

5. Fred's vision for his business was to eventually expand into Pacific Rim countries where cable television was in its infancy. Thus, he traveled a great deal. He was away over half of the time. While Fred was away, he had designated a management committee to be in charge, comprised of the chief financial officer, the vice president of construction and

the vice president of operations—affectionately referred to as the "Troika." Since a power struggle existed among the Troika, they seldom met. They each just "did their thing."

6. Significant quantities of electronic equipment had been ordered and delivered, which were inappropriately specified. They were for electronic signal frequencies other than what the company needed to complete the signal delivery system. They were custom built with lengthy lead-time requirements.

7. Planning and coordination between the construction division and operations division were virtually nonexistent. I suspected a full-blown contest was in force to see who could make the other look the worst. Both sides had made significant strides toward winning.

This sounds pretty messy. I often wonder how some businesses survive as long as they do. This was one of them. The most significant survival contributor in this case is item number four—no competition. In a normal competitive environment, this company would have disappeared. Fortunately, this "buffer" gave me time to get the business organized and running effectively, and then we sold the company to one of the major cable companies at a price too good to refuse. Here are the more significant actions I took to get the company on track.

1. Established the Executive Team. I reorganized the company from the existing three divisions into six divisions with six executives reporting to me. I worked with each one to make sure we had the people who could respond quickly to what needed to be done. This was not a complicated turnaround. It involved applying basic business practices to which most of these people had not been introduced. I only had to replace one of the players—he was incapable of making the necessary transition.

2. <u>Started Intensive Mentoring</u> For well over a year, I spent at least two hours per week training the executive team in basic management practices. Another two to three hours per week per person involved one-on-one coaching, which helped to overcome the major business knowledge deficit. An effective executive team is not an overnight phenomenon. It takes concentrated focus, month after month. In the two and a half years I worked with this company, a pretty good team emerged. They came a long way and earned good placements in the larger business entity after the acquisition.

3. <u>Implemented a Strategic Plan.</u> People were just showing up, day after day, responding to crises of their own making. After a short course on how to develop a strategic plan and an implementation plan, we started to systematically execute them. This was probably the most significant change process. People quickly caught on that we now had direction and we were in charge rather than always reacting to problems of the day.

4. <u>Supplier Meetings</u>. The supplier "loans" was one of the thorniest issues. In one scenario, our attorney and a contract had to neutralize the damage. For the remainder, a payment plan and a promise were necessary. It took a relationship-building meeting a professional CEO (me) who apologized for the situation and explained how it would be corrected and not repeated. The cure was not instantaneous, nor was that the expectation. After a few months of meeting our committed payment schedules, we got back to a semblance of normalcy in the supplier relationships.

My leadership in this process was not rocket science. I had the right training and experience for that job, and I had received the right preparation for the responsibilities I assumed. I achieved the business goals. My colleagues in the cable company had not been prepared for their jobs. They were failing. Essentially, the difference was the right knowledge. I continue to be struck by how many companies could significantly improve their business results if they decided to invest in training people to perform their responsibilities. I compare this situation to hiring a skilled craftsman then only providing him with a hammer.

Larger companies, generally when they reach the $100-$150 million threshold, see the need to hire a human resources professional. Then we usually, but not always, see an advocate for the value of training. Smaller companies, usually led by an entrepreneur, have not yet discovered the need, nor the benefits, of a well-trained cadre of workers.

Thus, I see a great need for businesses to have access to knowledge that can be absorbed quickly that communicates the essence of the best business practices. The goal should be to get the students in the game immediately using that knowledge and adding to it.

Championship Performance—Best Business Practices Development

My colleagues and I have found concentrated training sessions, based on best business practices related to building championship performance, to be the most effective team development process. We conduct specific training sessions designed to facilitate successful, refocused, executive team performance. This is the way we help companies build business intellectual capital.

Fundamentally, the development process mirrors that of professional athletes learning the team playbook. Management training is focused on a "playbook" containing distilled summaries of best business practices. This enables the participants to quickly embrace sufficient knowledge to start using it with their colleagues in their own businesses. Each "play" examines *why* the particular knowledge is important, *what* it looks like when being deployed, and *how* to put it to work.

Preparation

Years of experience by our senior staff in helping companies change from poor performers to successful performers led to several very significant conclusions. First is the need for the management team to take a hard look at itself and ask, "Are we really prepared for what lies ahead?" The next question is, "What else can we do to be successful three to five years from now?"

Accordingly, the companies that are looking hard at themselves and evaluating the answers to these questions are emerging as new business sector leaders, and they will continue to be successful. Why? Because, they are prepared to change both individually and corporately.

The key to being a continually successful company is based on a strategy of preparedness. Preparedness resides in getting the company's human resources ready to operate at peak levels. Having the right knowledge—and using it—is essential to top performance.

Building Greatness—The Right Culture

While this sounds like a great idea, it is not without a cost. The cost I refer to here primarily is to the leaders—the CEO and his or her team. Their leadership is required to forge the kind of culture that supports and encourages people to give their very best. Remember Abraham Maslow's hierarchy of human needs? It's still valid.

Maslow's Hierarchy of Needs	Leadership Culture
Self-Actualization ⟶	Trust
Self-Esteem	Passion
Belonging	Courage
Safety & Security	Informality
Food, Water, & Shelter	Forgiveness
	Humor

Using Maslow's terms, people must have their highest needs met in order to commit to giving their job their all. People need to achieve "self-actualization," feeling good about contributing their best, that is, playing the game at their highest level. What kind of a culture supports that process? It starts with trust. Trust is the glue that binds people together in a "safe" environment that is predictable. They know that they can count on the leadership to be fair. Other qualities of a great leadership culture include passion, courage, informality, forgiveness, and humor. While there are others, these six attributes are foundational to creating the kind of performance culture that spawns greatness. Take a look at your business culture. Are you getting close to creating these attributes? Ask your employees; use a survey and find out where you are and what you need to work on. Greatness has a price. If success was easy, everyone would have it.

For Further Reading—Mentoring Material

Michael Gerber, *The E Myth* (New York: HarperBusiness, 1986).

Eliyahu M. Goldratt, *The Goal* (New York: North river Press, 1992).

Tom Peters, *Liberation Management* (New York: Macmillan, 1992).

Chapter 3
Building the Value of Your Business

"By three methods we may learn wisdom; first, by reflection, which is noblest; second, by imitation, which is easiest; and third, by experience, which is the most bitter."
—Confucius

- Building Value
- The Use of Incentives
- Business Execution
- Management Intervention

Building Value

In most industries, it is now possible to acquire all the technology and hardware to compete in just about any marketplace. However, access to technology and equipment is not the differentiating factor. Differentiation comes from the ability to use it effectively. A company that loses all of its equipment but keeps the skills and know-how of its work force can be back in business fairly quickly. A company that loses its workforce but keeps all of its equipment can never recover. The effective use of knowledge and expertise is what creates greatness—not equipment.

The difference between physical and intellectual capital underscores a significant change in thinking about building greatness in any organization. In the last ten years trends in U.S. equity markets have reflected this shift. A significantly growing number of companies now rely on their intellectual capital as their source of competitive advantage. The application of knowledge is what creates the business advantage. Knowledge builds value in a company faster than any other strategy. Astute business leaders understand this phenomenon and have incorporated into their business strategies a process for building intellectual capital.

To underscore the increasing value of building know-how into a company's asset base, financial analysts on Wall Street are including intellectual capital in their business valuation models. In fact, a recent study of this trend reveals for the average analyst and portfolio manager 35% of his or her investment decision is supported by non-financial information. Following is a summary of the study, which highlights the top ten non-financial performance elements that affect the valuation of a company.

Top Ten Non-financial "Value Contributors"
Identified by Financial Analysts

Variable	Rank
Execution of corporate strategy	1
Management credibility	2
Quality of corporate strategy	3
Innovation	4
Ability to attract and retain talented people	5
Market share	6
Management expertise	7
Alignment of compensation with shareholder's interest	8
Research leadership	9
Quality of major business processes	10

Source: J. Low and T. Siesfield, *Measures That Matter*, Boston: Ernst & Young, 1998

The information in this report is striking for several reasons. Eight of these ten intangibles are affected by strategically focused HR development. The most important intangible cited is the ability to implement strategy. When you consider the impact of a well-executed strategy, you may well conclude that the ability to execute a strategy is as important as the strategy itself. Strategy execution is at the core of a company's ability to reinvent itself, which is exactly what businesses must be prepared to do to succeed in the current hyper-change business environment.

The Use of Incentives

A successful business strategy includes providing incentives for the behaviors you wish to reinforce, behaviors that reward performance while building value. We recommend that you develop the kind of incentives that address

- Base salary structure
- Short-term incentives
- Sales incentives
- Stock options
- Equity or equity-like long-term plans

Recently I discovered a new incentive idea from one of our colleagues in the wealth management business sector. His business is heavily dependent on providing highly specialized, knowledge-based advice. The incentives he has developed for his firm are significantly aimed at building knowledge and skills. Managers are rewarded for developing people. This is where you need to concentrate more of your incentive development. Building human resources is an essential element in increasing the value of your business. A well designed knowledge-building program, aimed at preparing the business to compete more effectively in the future, is the best step toward that goal.

Another incentive program that has been receiving quite a bit of attention, is highlighted in Jack Welch's new book, *Jack: Straight from the Gut*. Welch relates a story about a salary bonus he received early in his GE career. Three of his colleagues, with whom he shared an office, received the same level of bonus. Welch almost quit because he felt his contributions were at a much higher level based on the accomplishments he had posted. It was resolved by his boss's boss but not without a strong feeling that the compensation system was imbalanced. Welch held on to that conclusion until he had an opportunity to do something about it later in his meteoric career. With help from his HR colleagues, he developed the Differentiation—Vitality Curve. It was based on the belief that a group of managers can be divided into tiers based on levels of contribution. Thus, in a group of twenty managers, 20% (four) would be "A's," 70% (fourteen) would be "B's," and the bottom 10% (two) would be "C's." Here is a brief overview:

Differentiation – Vitality Curve

Group	%	Characteristics	Bonus
A	20	• Passion • Creative • Energizers • Exceed expectations • Self-developing	2-3 X
B	70	• Heart of the company • Trainable • Late bloomers • Committed	1-1.5 X
C	10	• Can't get job done • Enervative • "Don't get it" • Up or out	-0-

---

Welch reports that he pushed very hard to apply the program with vigor and toughness. He was determined to elevate the quality of people at GE. The rules were to love the A's—reward and further develop; try to make the B's into A's—smaller rewards but more development focus; and help the C's become B's—but if they could not make it, they had to go. He was insistent that each manager had to identify his or her bottom 10% and work to move them up or out.

While it may seem somewhat stern in the Welch application, the approach has significant merit in placing a strong emphasis on the manager's responsibility to assess and develop his or her employees. This is a behavior that needs to be emphasized strongly in the small-to-medium size business sector. Time and time again we find low-level business performance essentially attributable to lack of knowledge—and it takes a heavy toll.

Business Execution
Take note of some business performance research conducted by the Balanced Scorecard Collaborative, Inc., as reported in *Fortune* magazine. Their findings indicate that *less than 10% of strategies effectively formulated are effectively executed.* That is daunting. The conclusion is that most businesses are missing the opportunity to achieve greatness by simply not focusing on improving their

own business performance. And how can that be changed? Through a well-designed and well-executed strategy of HR development that focuses on the best business practices.

This is not a new trend in business. Peter Drucker, a national treasure for his contribution to the progress of U.S. business over the past 50 years, identified this important strategy over 25 years ago in his book, *The Practice of Management*. He identified that the first function of management is economic performance. He penned the great quote, "only excellence earns a profit," then explained the process involves management's responsibility to make a productive enterprise out of human and material resources. He also advised that to create the best business results, managers need to be responsible for:

- Setting objectives
- Organizing
- Motivating and communicating
- Measuring
- Developing people

A very large number of managers bear the title but have had very little preparation to carry out a manager's responsibilities. The propensity in business is to promote individuals into a management position based on their performance as non-managers! It happens all the time and the results are usually less than sterling. Opportunities are missed!

Let's take the management know-how "shortfall" one step further. Drucker points out in *The Practice of Management* that 20% of a manager's responsibility is developing people. How many managers do you know who spend 20% of their time developing their people?

Management Intervention
If you want to build a world-class business and achieve greatness in the process, your efforts must be supported, maybe even driven, by significant HR development. The most effective means of

building a world class organization is most effectively accomplished through a comprehensive mentoring program—carried out by the leaders within the business.

Unfortunately, I don't see an abundance of CEOs telling their colleagues what great results have been created by their mentoring program or their HR development program. While teaching CEOs may not be a broad-based phenomenon, there are some outstanding big successes, like Jack Welch at GE, Andy Grove at Intel, or Roger Enrico at PepsiCo. These successful leaders have called themselves "teaching CEOs." (Noel Tichy, *The Leadership Engine*). And, in their respective organizations, they have placed a huge emphasis on developing other leaders/teachers. They have been mentor-leaders. The process has created greatness. Consider these points in communicating an important business practice:

1. why this particular practice is important,
2. what it looks like in action, and
3. how to put it to work—education, application, and implementation!

The above material addresses education, point number one, underscoring the importance to the business of developing people.
The next chapter introduces the best business practices as a place to focus your people to create greatness.

For Further Reading—Mentoring Material

Brian Friedman, *Effective Staff Incentives* (London: Kogan Page, 1990).

Michael Porter, *Competitive Advantage* (New York: Macmillan, 1985).

Jack Welch with John Byrne, *Jack; Straight From the Gut* (New York: Warner Books, 2001).

Chapter 4
Best Business Practices

"A man's judgement is no better than his information."
—Chinese Proverb

- What Drives Performance Excellence?
- Six Disciplines of Championship Performance
- Best Business Practices
- Common Characteristics of Businesses at Risk
- Performance Capability Questions

What Drives Performance Excellence?

If asked, every business leader responds that he or she wants his or her business to be a top performer. But what does it take? Ask ten people, and you will get ten varied responses. The lack of real clarity is based in unconscious incompetence. Many people, filling responsible positions in business, do not know what they do not know that impacts their business performance. So, they are at risk—risk of not being a top performer or of not being able to stay in the game.

Our research involved examining successful organizations, looking at the practices that consistently delivered superior performance. It was not random; it was not accidental. Superior performance is the result of a well-studied strategy, competently and systematically executed. Our research and development team was comprised primarily of CEOs, former CEOs, and senior executives with business turn-around experience. Our objective was to identify the business practices that support consistent, predictable positive business results in the small-to-medium size business sector (under $250 million).

We factored out fortuitous events, being in the right place at the right time, and one-of-a-kind phenomena. Our quest was to identify the best practices employed by continuously successful companies in today's environment. These are the practices we found that significantly increase the predictability of successful results. However, first we identified the performance areas within which the best business practices can be summarized. We have called these performance areas the Six Disciplines of Championship Performance.

Six Disciplines of Championship Performance

By examining the performance drivers of successful companies we have identified six performance areas that are consistently found in companies producing superior results. An explanation of each of these disciplines follows.

Six Disciplines of Championship Performance

1. Strategic Planning and Implementation
Strategy has never been more important than it is today. For companies to be successful they must have the processes and guidelines to achieve their goals. Executive teams must have the knowledge to develop a strategic plan and the discipline to execute that plan. Less than 10% of strategies effectively formulated are effectively executed. Bad execution is the primary cause of failed strategy. A strategic plan is not enough to assure success. Companies must have execution discipline; key metrics to track performance; and the ability to make timely, needed adjustments to their plan.

2. Financial Management

Managing a company's resources to achieve continuous, predictable profitability is the test of management. This is management's purpose—not just the finance department's job. It takes the wisdom and coordinated efforts of all of senior management to assure the enterprise is focused on creating top financial performance. Traditional accounting and financial reports only provide historical information about where you have been. Lead indicators, definitive cost information, financial modeling, and hierarchy of revenue generators are some of the tools that are needed to achieve successful financial management. To achieve great financial results, management needs to know the financial score-what's working and what's not.

3. Systematic Management

Corporations need to achieve predictable outcomes in order to be successful. It is important to understand how products and services create demand for specific activities that in turn drive the need for resources. This starts with how management has been prepared to manage the resources of the enterprise. Management must understand the key processes that drive performance. Healthy systems enable predictable successful performance. Further, systems need to be constantly improved—a quality necessity. Striving for the highest quality through continuous improvement, as a manager as well as an enterprise, will differentiate you from your competitors. Companies with superior performance know their systems. They have been documented and are being further refined through continuous improvement initiatives.

4. Leadership

Leadership starts from the top, but can't stop there. The soul of any corporate culture emanates from whoever is in the strongest position to guide the corporate beliefs, values, and practices. The most successful companies have high performance cultures with a sense of purpose beyond just making money. A healthy culture will result in positive behaviors that are conducive to achieving the desired performance. Leadership is one of those behaviors that is no longer associated solely with the senior management team of a company. It occurs in two distinctive steps at all levels of the organization: (1) when individuals anticipate and identify an opportunity to make something positive happen, and (2) then take the responsibility for the process and results.

5. Productive Performance Relationships
High-performance organizations have high-performance teams that achieve a state of effectiveness as cohesive productive units. Achieving such high performance requires leadership, a focused goal, training, and open communication. Each individual must build positive productive relationships to be successful as an individual and as a member of a team. Relationships are built out of a common understanding and acceptance of style and role differences.

6. Learning and Growth
The competitive edge tomorrow belongs to those who know how to inspire more productivity and excellence from individuals, while building high performance teams and a high-performance culture. This means development should occur at three levels: individually, as a team, and as a company. Given that all development is self-development, companies must understand the role and importance of self-leadership in this major cultural shift. Comprehensive organizational learning is at the heart of a dynamic, energized company. To compete in a hyper-change environment requires an organization to change in order to compete. Knowledge is the cornerstone for building a great company.

Best Business Practices
Within the six performance areas, we identified the best business practices that fostered championship performance. Also, we

selected what we believe to be the essential as well as the best practices per performance area. As you work with these best practices, be sure to review if they indeed meet your industry needs. While there may be some variation between industries, and we readily accept that others may develop some variations, the best practices identified here are a very good place to start an improvement initiative.

Best Business Practices

1. Strategic Planning and Implementation
   * Budget is integrated with strategic planning process.
   * Meaningful performance review meetings are held regularly.
   * Performance measures—lead indicators—have been developed for predicting results.
   * The company's vision is clear and shared.
   * Work projects are prioritized and aligned with the strategic plan.
   * Potential threats to the business have been identified along with possible off-set strategies.
   * New products and/or services are in development.
   * Regular strategy review sessions are held.
   * Performance measures of key functions (Key Performance Indicators) have been developed and are reviewed regularly.
   * Customer satisfaction is measured and managed. implementation tracking systems are in use.
   * Broad-based knowledge of how the company is doing is shared.

2. Financial Management
   * Accountability has been clearly established for financial results.
   * Quality financial information is used for decision-making.
   * Budget reports tie to strategic plan execution.

- Profitability is strongly emphasized.
- An effective cash management system is implemented.
- The budget is used as a dynamic management tool.
- Key financial performance indicators are used to assess future direction.
- An effective cost-management system is in practice.
- A broad understanding of the business's financial performance exists.
- The company has been effective in the implementation of financial strategies.
- Generally, resources are allocated to the highest profit-contributing activities.
- The financial system identifies the hierarchy of profits (most profitable to least profitable) for products and/or services.

3. Systematic Management
   - Standard systems and procedures are well documented.
   - Improvement initiatives have been developed around each significant business process.
   - Excellent performance forecasting capability is present.
   - Employees, including first-time managers, are trained to meet tomorrow's needs.
   - Customer requirements are translated to actual business targets.
   - The company has effective and reliable operating systems.
   - Building company value is emphasized.
   - Company personnel generally understand how business value is created.
   - The company has a strategy to continually improve key business processes.
   - The entire company emphasizes quality.
   - The company provides training on quality application and practice.

- Improvement teams are widely used.

4. <u>Leadership</u>
   - The company leadership has achieved a high level of effectiveness.
   - The company has assured that management person nel are trained in the management basics.
   - The leadership maintains a high level of commitment to each other's success.
   - A strong customer focus is in place.
   - Throughout the company, respect is emphasized.
   - The company leadership shares the business's objectives with all personnel. High performance earns rewards (monetary). High performance earns rewards (non-monetary).
   - The company consistently achieves its targeted results.
   - Generally, decision-making is shared.
   - Effective performance-assessment and feedback processes are in place.
   - Generally, effective communication starts with the leadership

5. <u>Productive Performance Relationships</u>
   - A high level of harmony exists among the company leaders.
   - The company operates with a high level of trust.
   - Generally, the company has high morale.
   - A high level of collaboration thrives in the company.
   - A high level of camaraderie is present.
   - The leadership is effective in using and managing constructive dissent.
   - Meetings are generally meaningful and productive.
   - The company is concerned about the well being of its human resources.
   - An atmosphere of mutual support and commitment exists.

- An atmosphere of aggressive helpfulness is apparent.
- Mutual support is expected.
- Healthy supplier/customer business relationships exist.

6. <u>Learning and Growth</u>
    - The company systematically invests in training.
    - Good knowledge of the competition and what to expect from them are encouraged.
    - Support for personal growth and education initiatives are in place.
    - Core knowledge competencies to remain competitive have been developed.
    - Critical knowledge of technology trends affecting the business is fostered.
    - Effective leadership traits are understood and encouraged at all levels.
    - Knowledge and training to be an effective manager is provided to new managers.
    - The company is commitment to personal mastery (building personal competence).
    - Personal growth targets are encouraged.
    - The company is committed to continuous learning.
    - Knowledge is shared.
    - Knowledge is targeted for business development.

Common Characteristics of Businesses at Risk

A colleague with whom I sit on a board of directors, David, has commented on occasion that, "One is never as close to the edge as the bank may think and tell you that you are." David has now retired from a very successful career in which he was an expert at *edgemanship*. I value his insights. Nevertheless, I am amazed at the number of businesses that seem to keep muddling along, seemingly close to the edge, suffering from acute unconscious incompetence—not knowing what they don't know—that could make a big difference in their business results if they addressed their knowledge deficiencies.

Below I have identified some of the characteristics of companies we have considered at risk. I have categorized the symptoms by the six performance areas we consider significant for perpetuating and growing a business.

Characteristics of Businesses at Risk

1. Strategic Planning and Implementation
   - Limited vision of the future
   - Work force does not understand the strategy
   - Delinquent in implementing the strategic plan
   - Managers do not have incentives linked to strategy
   - Unaware of business opportunities
   - Decisions not evaluated in terms of impact on strategic plan
   - Unprepared for the unexpected

2. Financial Management
   - Budget and strategic plan not linked
   - Management information system consists of accounting system
   - No lead indicators
   - Hierarchy of revenue contributors unknown
   - No initiative for value creation
   - Lack of forecasting and modeling
   - Lack of financial accountability

3. Systematic Management
   - Lack of systems analysis capability
   - Lack of a champion for each system
   - Lack of systems documentation
   - Lack of continuous improvement initiative for systems
   - Lack of systems training
   - Projects initiated without a plan

- Low-impact operating systems

4. Leadership
   - Scarce application of shared leadership
   - Lack of decision making at the below corporate or team level
   - Uneven corporate direction
   - Risk-averse culture
   - Management succession unknown
   - Low morale/high turnover
   - Susceptibility to new management fads

5. Performance Relationships
   - Low utilization of teams and collaboration
   - Existence of turf wars
   - Colleagues treated as adversaries rather than partners
   - Low relationship skills
   - "Not my department/job"
   - Weak performance/reward culture
   - Lack of a sense of urgency

6. Learning and Growth
   - Budget cuts usually start with training
   - Core competencies unknown
   - No skill planning to support growth needs
   - Lack of learning incentives
   - Lack of understanding the impact of knowledge on company value
   - Managers appointed with no prior management training
   - Lack of performance benchmarks

The purpose of this mental search is to identify where to focus your energy to make your company more successful and resilient. That is leadership. Astute business leaders are addressing this issue and making a major commitment to stay in front of the knowledge curve. This means investing in people—making sure the right knowledge is being developed—and aggressively combating unconscious incompetence.

Let's see where your business may be in terms of utilizing some of the success-based practices discussed earlier. Consider the following series of questions as a mentoring opportunity.

Performance Capability Questions

1. Strategic Planning and Implementation
   - Are your business resources (people, money, and processes) fastidiously applied to the activities that will produce the preferred business results?
   - Are your strategies being carried out in everyday activities or are you constantly fire-fighting?
   - Are you taking what you get or getting what you want?

2. Financial Management
   - Is your business financial information clearly communicating how you are performing in the key areas?
   - Is your financial system supporting and driving performance?
   - Are you satisfied with your cash-flow management?

3. Systematic Management
   - Is your business performance predictable, giving you the comfort of knowing you have high probability of achieving excellent outcomes?
   - Are your operating systems well understood and designed to deliver optimal results?
   - Do you have an initiative to continuously improve your systems?

4. Leadership
   - Do people at all levels in your organization anticipate and identify opportunities to make positive contributions to your business results and then take responsibility to make those contributions? Are people being

prepared to manage more responsibility or are managers just given more responsibility?
- Are people trained to be manager-leaders or just appointed?

5. <u>Productive Performance Relationships</u>
- Are your people "at war" or do they treat each other like customers?
- Are your human resources working collaboratively to produce the very best results?
- Are productive relationships left to chance?

6. <u>Learning and Growth</u>
- If knowledge is the business weapon for future success, are your troops going to win or lose?
- Is your intellectual capital growing, according to a plan, to enable you to compete at a higher level?
- Do you have a strategy for the development of intellectual capital?

For Further Reading—Mentoring Material

Gary Hamel and C. K. Prahalad, *Competing for the Future* (Boston: Harvard Business, 1994).

Gordon Pearson, *The Competitive Organization* (New York: McGraw-Hill, 1992).

Chapter 5
Putting Mentoring to Work

"True leadership must be for the benefit of the followers, not the enrichment of the leaders."
—Robert Townsend

- Internal Development
- Commitment to Mentoring
- The Purpose of Mentoring
- What to Mentor
- Managers as Mentors
- The Manager Mentoring Process
- Mentoring-at-Large
- Mentoring/Coaching CEO's

Internal Development

Mentoring is *facilitating, guiding, and encouraging continuous innovation, learning, and growth.* It is a specific strategy for the development of intellectual capital that usually involves a leader/teacher from within the business itself. This goes to the core of the value of the mentoring process. Managers must develop their subordinates. Who better knows what kind of development should be taking place than a particular employee's manager? Most organizations don't seem to know how to get managers to mentor their subordinates, which is why many companies need the intervention of an outside facilitator.

I used to differentiate between mentoring and coaching, believing that coaching is usually more skill or curriculum oriented while mentoring is broader, more free-form. I have had to adjust my definition. I am seeing a lot of valuable free-form coaching. I conclude the line between mentoring and coaching has gotten a bit fuzzy. Whatever you call it, mentoring is a valuable and critical process that makes a significant impact on human resource (intellectual capital) development.

The biggest hurdle for most business leaders is not understanding how to mentor—so they don't. It's easier to send someone away to a course or seminar. Occasionally this can meet a need, but on the whole, the greatest impact on building intellectual capability and functionality within a business comes from within. Here are a few reasons why mentoring works.

Why Mentoring Works!

1. New knowledge can be developed with a view toward how it can be used to help create positive results for the company.

2. People in a business, learning together, dramatically increase the probability that the knowledge will be used in the business (compared to individuals going away for a course).

3. Leaders learning how to be effective mentors mobilize a powerful development process.

4. A company's ability to stay in the game depends on what it knows, how it uses what it knows, and how quickly it can learn something new. Strategic mentoring can deliver the needed support to sustain targeted, continuous learning.

5. Mentoring direct reports enables the mentor to focus on specific and strategic growth opportunities.

6. An internal mentoring program can support the building of a performance-oriented culture.

7. Mentors must continue to learn in order to be effective; thus, they are modeling and supporting continuous learning.

8. With training, all managers can be mentors.

Commitment to Mentoring

A well-conceived and well-executed mentoring program is based on and sustained by commitment that starts from the top and permeates the organization. Commitment is preceded by a thoughtful and comprehensive evaluation. To achieve the benefits, a thorough implementation process must be followed. To achieve a successful program, a company normally starts with an assessment of the costs—and benefits, followed by a change-management process. A change-management check list is provided in the next chapter.

The Purpose of Mentoring

Generally, a business launches a mentoring program based on the belief that it is an effective means of building human resource competencies, thus, building overall value. Although I have seen numerous motives, they usually involve building performance capability. Variations on the process are based on perceived need and benefit. One of my clients' mentoring program places emphasis on pairing individuals—volunteer mentors are matched to volunteer mentees. This works for special purpose mentoring programs aimed at supporting overall career development and growth. I could describe numerous variations on this theme. This has value and probably represents the majority of mentoring initiatives. However, my own experience with assisting clients with mentoring has evolved to recommending a more focused approach. It involves a game plan that builds the business's performance capability through concentrating on best business practices. It parallels a sports team working on the plays that build their performance prowess. In business, to succeed, you must work on the plays or practices that will yield top performance, hence, best business practices.

The CEO must be a strong proponent and practitioner for a mentoring program to succeed. When the CEO drives and models it, mentoring will become part of the culture. Then, the program not only works but makes a significant contribution to business performance and even morale. It creates "the performance energizer," putting the focus on the right stuff.

What to Mentor?

The three high priority mentoring areas are as follows:

- Personal skills to enhance performance
- Career development
- Best business practices

1. Personal skills

Mentoring or coaching personal skills is one of the more common applications in HR development. Personal coaches or mentors can speed up the development process and facilitate getting individual capabilities to a higher level thereby enabling someone to play the game at a higher level—faster. Personal skill areas could include some of the following:

- Communication skills such as public speaking and report writing
- Project management skills
- Effective meeting techniques
- Time management
- Specific job skills such as strategic planning and workplan implementation
- Performance short-falls and growth areas

2. Career development

Encouraging colleagues to work on furthering their careers, in essence, is to urge continued growth and development. This includes completing college degrees, graduate work, certifications, licenses, and the like.

3. Best business practices

As discussed in the preceding chapter, mentoring the best business practices represents a great opportunity to align intellectual capital development with high-value benefits. Our approach is to identify the best practices that include the essential business knowledge that will reach the greatest number of common business needs. Your list may vary a bit from ours. That's okay. The goal is to accommodate and apply the best business practices to an organization's specific performance needs.

All three areas are important and should be addressed. Yet, the greatest payoff to the business is the third area—mentoring best business practices—and it usually gets the least attention. That is where you should place the emphasis for two reasons. First, there is overall benefit to everyone involved. Second, we can use a script focused on business improvement. Having meaningful content solves one of the common problems of not knowing *what* to start mentoring.

Building a knowledge base of the essential, fundamental business practices that can deliver better results has huge paybacks for the participants and the business. This knowledge will enable individuals to enhance their careers by becoming more effective in helping their company achieve a higher level of success. Ultimately, that's what the market is looking for. In my book *MENTORING for Exceptional Performance*, based on years of organizational experience, I suggested the areas to concentrate on were *leading, learning and relationships*. Those were the areas where productive intervention could create the preferred results. That still holds. However, I now have added details specific to developing business performance capabilities.

Managers as Mentors

In an era of knowledge workers, managers have a significantly greater responsibility in the development of knowledge in their business environment. Managers need to learn how to be good mentors. A significant portion of a manager's time should be directed to the development of his or her direct reports. Some companies now offer incentives and reward managers for the intellectual capital—increased learning—they create. Training managers how to be good mentors is a significant value-building process. Let's take a look at such a program.

The Manager Mentoring Process/Hierarchy

The mentoring process involves establishing a hierarchy of mentor-mentee meetings. It involves expanding a manager's regular supervisory meetings with a direct report into a network of focused mentoring/development sessions. The steps are as follows:

Institutionalizing Mentoring

1. Select and commit to regular meetings.

2. The mentee is responsible for preparing the meeting agenda. The agenda should include, but not be limited to the following:

  - Items for which the mentee should provide progress updates, present information and/or seek guidance. This creates an opportunity for the mentee to have any question addressed, share concerns, or make observations. It's his or her dedicated, quality time with his or her supervisor/manager. The execution points related to the strategic plan would fit here.

  - Items the manager suggests during the week that he or she would like to discuss. This reduces the need for multiple, special meetings, which tend to disrupt concentration and take more time.

- Mentoring/growth topics that could be created by either party.

3. The agenda should be in the hands of the mentor at least one day in advance of the meeting. This gives the mentor an opportunity to reflect and prepare.

4. The mentee is responsible for developing and submitting the proposed mentoring plan to the mentor, which is to become a part of the one-hour, weekly meeting. The plan should be mutually developed with input from the mentor for specific growth content he or she observes would benefit the mentee.

5. The mentoring plan should cover at least a six-month period and contain specific goals and areas of development, with measurable milestones.

6. At least quarterly, the participants should evaluate how the meetings are progressing and what can be done to improve them.

7. When every manager adapts this meeting process, the organization will have a comprehensive network of management development, focused communication, and coordinated strategy execution. The organization will become networked with mentors and mentees as well as concentrated quality work focus.

8. Keep looking for ways to make it better.

Mentoring-at-Large
The one-on-one meetings are not the only mentoring opportunities. Some of your most effective mentoring sessions will be in small

groups/teams. The "aha" of mentoring is the bringing together of an issue, relevant knowledge, and application. This is true whether it's mentoring an individual, a team, or a whole organization. The fun and excitement are seeing the participants experience the "aha." The challenge to the mentor is to look for these kinds of opportunities. Consider the benefits you have in an organization with numerous mentors looking for such opportunities- it's powerful.

The most effective means for a mentor to create this process is to look for the right article, book, video—some form of transferring knowledge—on a current issue that could benefit your situation. Then, ask your colleague(s) to read the material, followed by a scheduled time to specifically consider what application(s) can be drawn for your particular issues. The opportunity can be summarized in three words: *education, application,* **and** *implementation!*

When creating these "aha" sessions, make them informal and light. You will see some astonishing break-throughs in an informal, relaxed, off-site get-together. Various forms of barriers and resistance will be minimized when you can relax the setting and the relationships among the participants. Getting people to relax and work in a more flexible, informal setting seems to enable the release of more creativity as well. A thoughtful mentor creates these situations.

By now you can see that an effective mentor has to constantly be on the lookout for knowledge to share. That is the beginning point of the process. Our challenge in creating greatness is to get as many mentors committed to continuous learning, gathering knowledge, and creating as many "aha" experiences as possible.

Mentoring/Coaching CEOs

A growing trend for CEOs is to be the recipients of personal mentoring or coaching. In today's rapidly changing business environment, many CEOs have not had the time to address their own development as much as they would like—or should! Yet their leadership is crucial to the success of the enterprise they head. How can a business post championship results if the leadership is not at the championship level?

From my speaking engagements, consulting, and working with venture capital and investment banking firms, I come into contact with a lot of CEOs. I have met many CEOs who have not realized that they have an opportunity to improve the performance of their business by adding basic business management information to their own knowledge base.

An interesting phenomenon in small-to mid-size businesses is that the CEO and senior management usually are very competent in the technical knowledge of their industry. However, they assume this will enable them to achieve successful business results. Just as so many managers who get appointed to management positions with little or no management training, the same can happen at the CEO level. CEOs usually have the technical knowledge—they are only missing the basic management knowledge that often means the difference between mediocrity and excellence in the performance of their business.

I really enjoy coaching a CEO who wants to be the best he or she can be. It's exciting when you encounter a CEO who has a good grasp of what he or she doesn't know about management and wants to do something about it. As a result of many CEOs being underprepared for their roles, I encounter many who are not enjoying their jobs nearly as much as they could or should. It's hard to enjoy performing when you are not adequately prepared.

After speaking at a senior executive business luncheon, a gentleman asked if I could answer a few questions for him. I said, "Sure, fire away." He introduced himself as Jim and said he had been a CEO for about six years and was looking for a few solutions to current problems he was facing. He followed up by asking me two questions: first how I became trained as a CEO and second, how I trained or coached other CEOs. I told him I would try to give him the brief version, which goes something like this.

For the first nine years after I graduated from college I worked for the city administrative officer in the city of Los Angeles. I worked in the management and budget office. For those nine years, I received very good training in performance budgeting and management analysis. I also received a full scholarship for my master's degree in administration, which I completed at night. During this time, wanting to improve my communication skills, I also taught a class in supervision at the local community college. Further, I was studying regularly for promotional exams. It was a time of intense learning. I discovered the value of learning and enjoyed it very much. I was promoted rapidly and enjoyed the increasing responsibility.

In my early thirties I competed for a position in Portland, Oregon as the first director of management services, which was the chief administrative officer responsible for the city's budget, finance and personnel functions. I got the job. This was a new department. I worked with the mayor and city council and we virtually invented the new department. The newly elected mayor, Neil Goldschmidt, was thirty years old. (Neil later became secretary of transportation under President Jimmy Carter as well as governor for the state of Oregon). What an incredible time we had. In our youthful vigor and enthusiasm to make a contribution, we did not realize what we could not do. So we did a lot. Certainly not having all the answers, I sought out an advisor, someone who could mentor me through the difficult issues I encountered in this position.

I networked through several senior managers I knew until I found an advisor who became my mentor. His name is John Olsen. I could fill pages telling of John's wonderful insights and wisdom he shared with me. John was an incredible resource. For thirty years John has been at the other end of the phone whenever I need him. He significantly contributed to my understanding of the importance of knowledge and responsibility and opportunity of being the "chief knowledge officer" in leading a cadre of knowledge workers. Further, Mayor Goldschmidt was one of the brightest men I had ever met and attracted the same. For example, he called me at home one Friday night (not an uncommon event) and asked me if I would like to join him for breakfast the next morning with former Oregon Senator Wayne Morris and author John Kenneth Galbraith. Neil loved to spring these learning opportunities on his colleagues.

A few years later, I was recruited into the private sector, which started my journey through eight very different CEO positions. The various opportunities usually involved a major transition—a turn-around, merger, start-up, or sale. All have involved vast amounts of change, building executive teams and growing knowledge. I became committed to a lifetime of learning, which usually means reading fifty to sixty books a year as well as the usual journals and periodicals. Learning is exciting, primarily because it has allowed me to participate in the game of business, and life, as much more than an observer. I have been able to play the game at a very exciting level.

I also added that I found that I am a teaching CEO, mentoring and coaching my business colleagues. That required me to always be on the lookout for material to add to my mentoring curriculum. I did this because I had made a major discovery: The more we—the executive team—learned about the process of building excellence into our company, the better the business results.

Jim asked me how the managers usually felt about all the extra learning. "Didn't they find it awfully time consuming?" I replied that that often had been mentioned at the outset. But I found ways to start the process that can be enjoyable and engaging. I always start where the learners are. Don't bombard them with your enthusiasm. Let them see the benefits of acquiring knowledge that will contribute to their performance and their appetite will develop.

I then tried to answer the second major question Jim framed at the outset, "How do you mentor or coach other CEOs?" I explained that my commitment to be a lifetime learner as a CEO had created a focus on what successful CEOs and successful companies do. What are the processes and practices that produce predictable success? The content of what I have developed essentially are the best business practices presented in the second part of this book.

How I coach a CEO looks something like this:

1. We set a meeting to explore what it is the CEO is looking to accomplish in his or her business. I ask the CEO to
think about these questions and be prepared to share his or
her answers to the following questions with me:

    a. Are you confident you are doing everything possible
        to create successful business results in your
        company?
    b. What is your model? Describe your leadership
        modus operandi—how do you lead and develop
        your executive staff?
    c. What three issues are of most concern right now?

2. From the first meeting, we decide on a direction for a
coaching process. It can take two forms:

Form A—Work only with the CEO. This form
involves two phases. First, we develop a meeting
schedule for a two-to-four-hour coaching session
(face-to-face or viatelephone), once or twice a
month, depending on the CEOs time commitment.
The CEO prepares the agenda of issues and problems to work on. I add suggested items and provide
learning material as we progress through the coaching agenda. The objective for these sessions is to
address the specific areas the CEO identifies as concerns and work on those. The second phase is to
assess where the CEO is in general application of
the best basic business practices. Based on the
results, we will outline an agreeable coaching
program.

Form B—Work with the CEO and his or her executive team. This usually includes all of Form A above
plus coaching the CEOs executive team. The coaching is based on an assessment of the team in their

understanding and application of the best business practices. The objective is to work with the CEO to help him or her lead the knowledge development process with his or her team. The CEO should become the knowledge leader. The training sessions with the whole team are designed around education, application, and implementation.

I explained to Jim that a coaching engagement can last for six months, a year, or longer, depending on the CEO's needs. Jim inherited his business (specialized optical measurement equipment) from his father, although the ownership transfer is still in process. His father started the business after World War II and built it to a $70 million company six years ago when Jim took over as CEO; they are now at $110 million in annual revenue. Jim has an MBA and good knowledge of his industry but had not had a CEO model in his father that he could pattern his performance after. His father had been the classic entrepreneur who delegated very little and was skilled at making most of the important decisions in the company. Jim was moving the company toward a shared leadership model and wanted to build his executive team to achieve 15% annual growth or better. Jim became a client.

At this writing, Jim has moved quickly into his role as knowledge leader. I provide him with "knowledge material" such as articles from business periodicals, book excerpts, and the like that highlight a potential business application for his business. Jim distributes it to his team prior to a "work-out meeting." A "work-out" consists of taking a bit of new knowledge and having the team evaluate:

1. Why is this important?
2. What does it look like in use?
3. Can we see some value in its application in our business?

Jim and his team are also targeting a business acquisition that should enable them to comfortably achieve their 15% annual growth goal for the next few years.

Part of my coaching process is focused on helping the CEO become the knowledge leader for his or her company. Successful companies of the future will be learning organizations, taking on new knowledge that puts them in the forefront of their business sector. One of the most effective means to build knowledge, while building a strong performance culture, is through team learning. CEOs lead this important process, which is particularly effective in simultaneously adding shareholder value while building the intellectual capital of his or her company. In the next chapter, you will learn how to initiate a mentoring program in your business.

For Further Reading—Mentoring Material

Chip R. Bell, *Managers as Mentors* (San Francisco: Berrett-Koehler, 1996).

Robert Hargrove, *Masterful Coaching* (San Diego: Pfeifer & Company, 1995).

Harold E. Johnson, *MENTORING for Exceptional Performance* (Glendale: Griffin, 1997).

Davis Megginson and Davis Clutterbuck, *Mentoring in Action* (London: Kogan Page, 1995).

Eric Parsloe, *Coaching, Mentoring and Assessing* (London: Kogan Page, 1992).

Chapter 6
Initiating a Mentoring Program

"I've always believed that if you put in the work, the results will come. I don't do things halfheartedly. I know if I do, then I can expect halfhearted results."
—Michael Jordan

- Mentor-Leaders
- Change Management
- Business Intelligence
- Just-In-Time Knowledge
- Selection of JIT Knowledge

Mentor-Leaders

Consider the term "workleader" created by author Emmet Murphy in his book, *Leadership IQ*. Workleaders are workers who lead and leaders who work. Well, let's borrow a page from Mr. Murphy's book and consider what a "mentor-leader" might look like. Assume they will be committed to take the lead in innovation, learning and growth. Mentor-leaders are not necessarily top-level managers or possibly not managers at all. They could be research and development specialists, IT (information technology) technicians or mail room strategists. All can participate in the process of making the business more successful. This is where self-leadership becomes important.

Everyone in the organization can be involved in continuous learning—if he or she chooses to. This is a mega-opportunity for the business leadership. When you get all of your employees committed to growth and learning, you have created a most powerful force in your business. But it will not happen by itself. The business leadership must create the culture that underscores the benefits and rewards of learning and growth—"what's in it for me" (WIIFM).

Change Management

Introducing a new program into an organization is not a process to be taken lightly. It takes planning and execution to be successful. Unfortunately, many businesses have too much "scar tissue." A number of programs, often referred to as the "flavor of the month," get introduced poorly and die an agonizing death. This is a waste of time and energy, while at the same time eroding management credibility. And it happens frequently in many organizations. Following is a studied process for successfully introducing change.

Introducing change can be accomplished effectively with focused forethought and planning. Difficulties in implementing change come not from misunderstanding *what* to do but from a lack of understanding *why* and *how* to do what needs doing. Take a look at a checklist for change developed at GE. This checklist now has been used in some form for thousands of change projects at hundreds of companies.

Keys and Processes for Making Change Happen

Key Success Factor for Change	Questions for Assessing and Accomplishing Change
1. Leading change (who is responsible?)	Do we have a leader… • who owns or champions the change? • who demonstrates public commitment to make it happen? • who will garner resources to sustain it? • who will invest personal time and attention following it through?

2. Creating a shared need (why do it?)

Do employees...
• see the reason for the change?
• understand why the change is important?
• see the benefits for them and/or the business?

3. Shaping a vision (what will it look like when we are done?)

Do employees...

• see the outcomes of the change in behavioral terms (what will they do differently as a result of the change)?
• get excited about these outcomes?
• understand how the change will benefit customers and other stake holders?

4. Mobilizing commitment (who else needs to be involved?)

Do sponsors of the change...

• recognize who else needs to be committed to the change for it to happen?
• know how to build a coalition of support for the change?
• have the ability to enlist the sup port of key individuals in the organ-ization?
• have the ability to build a respon-sibility matrix to make the change happen?

5. Building enabling systems (how will it be institutionalized?)

Do sponsors of the change...

• understand how to sustain the change through modifying HR sys-tems (e.g. staffing, training, appraisal, rewards)?
• recognize the technology invest-ment required to implement the change?
• have access to financial resources to sustain the change?

| 6. Monitoring and demonstrating progress (how will it be measured?) | Do the sponsors of the change....

• have a means of measuring the success of the change?
• plan to benchmark progress on both the results of the change and the implementation process? |
| 7. Making it last (how will it be initiated and sustained?) | Do the sponsors of the change....

• recognize the first steps needed to get started?
• have a short- and long-term plan to keep attention focused on this plan?
• have a plan for adapting the change over time to shifting circumstances? |

Brian Becker, Mark Huselid, and Dave Ulrich, *The HR Scorecard* (Harvard Business School Press, 2001).

Implementing a mentoring program begins with identifying the champion—the person with the interest, ability, and authority to make it happen. This requires full support and participation from the CEO or COO. Getting the board's blessing and acceptance is important as well.

Next, appoint a steering committee from various levels of the organization. This increases the likelihood of understanding implementation issues throughout the organization as well as developing broad-based acceptance and support. The champion should chair the steering committee. One of the first exercises for the steering committee is to spend the time to thoroughly consider the above Checklist for Change. This will be of great assistance in developing an implementation plan. The better the implementation plan and execution, the better the results.

Evaluating what successful companies have done is valuable. No one approach is best. Each company has different circumstances, conditions, aspirations, and even levels of commitment. The best advice is anything worth doing is worth doing well. Initial training, followed by evaluation, planning, and conscientious implementation can create and support exceptional results. And that is what successful businesses do.

Business Intelligence

Having effective business intelligence materials, such as targeted, concise reports, and topical papers, contribute to identifying significant improvement opportunities. In this process, the team is trained in the use of the management processes that support successful business performance. The process includes team learning and application, following the formula of education, application, and implementation. The process involves

• Just-in-Time (JIT) Knowledge
This describes a streamlined version of the learning and application process. The essential knowledge covering a critical element of successfully managing an enterprise has been reduced to a cogent, brief learning document. It is put to use immediately in a team environment.

• Best Practices Development
Many of today's business leaders come from backgrounds that have not provided training in core business practices. The best business practices—introduced in the next section—are what highly successful organizations use to create consistent, predictable, and preferred results.

• Immediate Implementation
The knowledge is applied immediately in the client's business in a workshop forum. The executive team actually works out the implementation process together after achieving a common understanding of the potential benefits of implementation.

Selection of JIT Knowledge

Essentially, the evolution of what material to use to address unconscious incompetence evolved from three sources. First, I have been a continuing student of management literature since graduating from college. Generally, I keep up with the current flavor of what my colleagues are sharing with business-oriented readers. While I agree with the wisdom literature found in the Book of Ecclesiastes—that there is nothing new under the sun—clever sorting and packaging of management thought and experience continues. This is helpful for the manager to maintain a healthy sense of what is going on with successful businesses.

Second, during my experiences as a transition CEO in various environments, I have found myself starting with an evaluation of my management team's strengths and weaknesses. I found out early in my career it is far better to surround yourself with truly capable colleagues. It makes the process of running a business much more pleasurable. So I developed an evaluation-assessment process to see if my colleagues could deliver what was needed for predictably successful outcomes. Then I followed up with the intervention learning process (*Critical Knowledge Summaries*) to fill in knowledge gaps, which would address performance gaps. From this process, I developed an overall basic management curriculum I expected our managers to master. As a teaching CEO, this offers so many wonderful culture building opportunities that enhance the high performance attitude a CEO likes to see in his or her company.

The third source really is a refinement of the second one. As I began to see the wisdom and effectiveness of getting my management teams involved in continuous learning—and learning the right stuff—it was a logical extension to concentrate on refining the process. That led to researching the various methodologies of evaluating executive performance against the relevant criteria. That evolved into the Six Disciplines of Championship Performance described in chapter four.

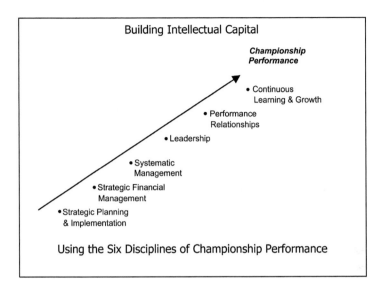

Then it was a matter of developing a process of making this critical knowledge as accessible as possible so it can be put to work immediately. Thus, the *just-in-time* designation. You should be looking for knowledge that can make a difference, and then put it to work right away. Get it and use it. Then start evaluating what you need to do or know next to make it better.

Some clients have not been shy about saying they just don't have time to read to get new knowledge. While I know they are busy, I believe a lot of people either do not know how to use their time effectively or they are not motivated. It is a busy time we live in, and I know it is not easy to juggle all the demands and segregate that quiet time for additional knowledge—unless you are really motivated or you have discovered how to wedge that bit of time for reading into your schedule. Ultimately, those who do read consistently have learned how to prioritize. They know they have to if they are going to continue to develop their career.

Knowledge is where every process starts, and it needs to be the right knowledge—knowledge that can be taken on board, then applied in a common-sense way to start making a positive difference.

The next section contains eight chapters that describe *how* to mentor knowledge based on the best business practices in six championship performance areas.

For Further Reading—Mentoring Material

Karl E. Sveiby, *The New Organizational Wealth—Managing and Measuring Knowledge-Based Assets* (San Francisco: Berret-Koehler, 1997).

Daniel R. Tobin, *Transformational Learning—Renewing Your Company Through Knowledge and Skills* (New York: John Wiley & Sons, 1996).

Part II

What to Mentor

Chapter 7

Getting Started—Best Business Practices

"Motivation is what gets you started.
Habit is what keeps you going."
—Jim Ryun

- How to Use This Material
- First Steps
- The Mentoring Grid
- Mentoring Content
- Mentoring Application

How to Use This Material

Too many top-level managers are taking advantage of a very small portion of the management wisdom available to them. Unconscious incompetence is still a major contributor to low-level business success. The following material will enable the reader to access some of the basic wisdom that, when applied diligently, significantly increases the odds for improved performance.

The challenge to the mentor-leader is to find creative and effective ways to introduce new knowledge to his or her colleagues. In fact, it doesn't have to be new knowledge; it can be a review of the basic business knowledge most managers should know. What you are looking for are the answers to "What can you do better?" Leaders in successful businesses engage their colleagues in a search for excellence as part of the corporate culture. That suggests we are on a continuous quest for improvements. That sounds good, and it is good, as far as it goes. The mentor-leader has the great opportunity to prime the pump.

Where do good ideas, even break-through ideas, come from? Usually they are the result of a focused search. Herein lies a major opportunity for the mentor-leader. You can help set the stage for the growth and application of knowledge. You can be the catalyst for knowledge growth and application. This is what great companies and great leaders are spawning.

First Steps

Here are a few suggestions on how to take advantage of this material in your organization:

- Form a book discussion group, assign one chapter per session, and examine what could be done better by applying the principles in your organization.

- Once a month during a staff meeting, lead a discussion where each member reads selected material in advance and comes prepared to discuss improvements.

- Hold a retreat and assign material to be read in advance and discuss at the retreat. Then form special focus groups to evaluate new opportunities.

- As part of the annual strategic planning process review some pertinent material and conduct a "What can we do better?" evaluation session.

- As part of a promotion evaluation, require each candidate to read the material and write a paper on "What we can do better in our organization."

The important aspect of continued business success is continuous improvement. And everyone needs to be involved. What Else Can We Do? is the battle cry—but you can't play a good game if you are not prepared. A good friend of mine is on the board of directors of one of the National Football League teams. He said the team has one coach for every 2.3 players. And the team has been to the Super Bowl four times in eleven years. I believe mentoring can help facilitate a business team's vision for greatness and help them get there. After over thirty years of looking for effective ways to accelerate top-level performance, I am convinced mentoring is the pathway to building greatness in a business.

The Mentoring Grid

The best business practices embrace leading, learning, and relationship skills as the performance-delivery knowledge that enables top-level performance. Add to that the specific operational knowledge, which includes strategic planning and implementation, financial management, and systematic management. Add to the formula that the knowledge should be mentored to individuals, teams, and the culture for maximum benefit. This produces an implementation grid that looks like this:

Mentoring Implementation Grid
Best Business Practices

	Strategic Plan.	Financial Mgt.	System. Mgt.	Leadership	Relationships	Learning
Individual						
Team						
Culture						

The mentoring strategy, then, should be to fill in all eighteen boxes with specific actions to enhance the business's performance. You can approach this in several ways, depending on the size of the organization. It can be developed by level, department, function, or location. The corporate mentoring champion must set the guidelines for optimum benefit and implementation success.

Following is an example from a client file. These strategies were developed by the executive team for the knowledge and understanding they wanted every manager to have.

Mentoring Targets

Strategic Planning and Implementation

Individual -   Understand the process of preparing a solid plan, with emphasis on the importance of disciplined implementation on a time ly basis.

Team -   Develop not only the planning process but how we can help each other get it accomplished with exceptional results.

Culture -   Understand what we as a company of knowledge workers are committed to accomplish and the importance of every person's contribution to the whole.

Financial Management

Individual -   Understand the basic elements of financial management—the importance of "knowing the numbers."

Team -   Keep an eye on the lead indicators to guide financial perform ance to the preferred results.

Culture -   Create a financial scoreboard to provide feedback on how we are doing as a company. Use to build awareness of the importance of each individual's contribution.

Systematic Management

Individual -   Understand systems and their importance in developing predictability and consistency of results.

Team -   Develop an ongoing improvement initiative for key systems and processes. Assure each system has a champion tasked with making it better.

Culture -   Develop an understanding of the importance of incremental improvement—"What else can we do to make it better?"

Leadership

Individual -   Understand the need to identify opportunities and take responsibility for results.

Team -   Share leadership with those who can make a contribution.

Culture -   Understand the stakeholder mindset—"How can I contribute to the success of our company?"

Relationships

Individual -	Understand that constructive, positive working relationships are foundational to effective performance—each person is a major contributor to the performance ethic.
Team -	Model the effective process of teamwork—"Your success is my success."
Culture -	Treat each colleague as a customer—"How may I help you?"

Learning and Growth

Individual -	Understand that all development is self-development—"What do I need to learn to grow with my company?"
Team -	Model the knowledge growth process. Demonstrate commitment to continuous learning.
Culture -	Involve the leadership in facilitating knowledge development demonstrate importance through commitment from the top.

Mentoring Content

Let's take a look at what mentors can address in carrying out his or her responsibilities in their organization. The application as to individual, team, or culture would depend on the setting, business size, business decentralization, and so on. A mentoring plan should be developed with and for each direct report, with thought given to how it can be applied to the team as well as the culture. Here's an example of mentoring strategic planning implementation at these three levels:

- Individual—Specific project review sessions; use of progress briefings for feedback, guidance, and information exchange.

- Team—Regularly review progress of plan implementation, focusing on areas that impact several, if not all, members of the team; encourage collaboration to identify best outcomes; build support and understanding for each other'sarea of responsibility.

- Culture—Senior management mentors the culture by the level of commitment they demonstrate by their combined follow-through with strategic plan implementation through regular progress reviews, a collaborative reprioritization process, and generally, the support demostrated—"walking the talk."

Mentoring Application

The following chapters are focused on the six disciplines to improve overall corporate performance. Each has a number of specific contributing elements. The executive team should be involved in determining the overall direction, but someone must take the lead, and I suggest this be the CEO. Only systems and projects with a champion achieve their potential. In this endeavor, it works best if the champion is the CEO or possibly the COO.

However, I have a caution—don't overreach. Keep the mentoring effort practical and manageable. After selecting the highest pay-off objectives, the mentor should then evaluate how to mentor the individual, the team, and the culture. Keep it basic to start.

Go through the six performance disciplines looking for the opportunity for greatest benefit. Usually that means starting with your strategic planning and implementation process. Start here because you need to make sure the allocation and use of your resources are in alignment with where you want to take your business.

The material in the next chapters has the specific goal of identifying the methodology best followed to mentor an organization in each of the six specific performance disciplines. These guidelines and ideas will serve the mentor best if they represent the starting point. Please evaluate the material in terms of how you can best apply it and improve it in your specific business setting. It's an exciting and rewarding journey when the participants are focused on looking for the best business results. It is the best process I have found to get as many players in the game as possible, prepared and focused on playing to win.

For Further Reading—Mentoring Material

Gerrard Egan, *Adding Value—A Systematic Guide to Business-Driven Management and Leadership* (San Francisco: Jossey-Bass, 1993).

Michael Hammer, *The Agenda—What Every Business Must Do to Dominate the Decade* (New York: Crown Business, 2001).

Robert Kaplan and Davis Norton, *The Strategy Focused Organization* (Boston: Harvard Business, 2001).

Phil Lowe and Ralph Lewis, *Management Development Beyond the Fringe* (London: Kogan Page, 1994).

Chapter 8

Strategic Planning & Implementation

"Any enterprise is built by wise planning, becomes strong through common sense, and profits wonderfully by keeping abreast of the facts."
—Living Proverbs, 14:3,4

- Where Do You Want to Go Today?
- Strategy Makes the Difference
- What Succesful Companies Do
- Implementation!
- Implementation Planning
- Implementation Tracking
- Mentoring the Future You Want
- Getting Started—Education
- Application
- Mentoring Questions

Where Do You Want To Go Today?

Microsoft has a compelling approach to marketing their software, couched in terms of "where do you want to go today?" It's compelling in the sense that in the day-to-day duties that business managers face, you need to take a moment to think about where you are going. What are you trying to achieve, and how are you going to get there? After spending over thirty years helping business and government try to figure out where they are going and how they are going to get there, I conclude that there is an enormous opportunity to improve performance in this area.

Paradoxically, this is one of the most significant areas for mining value for an organization, yet one of the areas in which there is significant underachievement. The lack of thorough planning and implementation eventually creates a breeding ground for problems. More often than not, I work with the founder/CEO who has done a good job of building a business as a focused entrepreneur. However, now he or she is encountering some need to react to one of several significant issues that could be a threat to his or her business. The problem generally occurs as a result of the lack of anticipation and planning. The issues usually include one or more of the following:

- Changing marketplace
- Succession
- Growth
- Management

Most businesses get to this spot through what I call benign neglect, or, just showing up. Most businesses keep operating the way they always have—from crisis to crisis, project to project. The familiar is comfortable, so that seems to be where many CEO types reside. And it takes a significant event in the form of a formidable problem to start them looking for a different or better way forward.

Strategy Makes the Difference

Strategic thinking is essential to business success. Appreciating the potential value of a strategic plan is easier when the role and importance of strategy is understood.

Business leaders agree that strategic thinking is most likely to support the delivery of the best business results. But what happens after the intellectual recognition of its value continues to be a mystery. If it is so valuable in its contribution to business results, why is there such a low level of proficiency in doing it well?

Companies that succeed in today's rapidly changing and competitively tough business environment have learned how to effectively manage performance. It is an ongoing process in which organizations know the level of performance required to meet their strategic objectives and manage them continually. This ensures that objectives remain relevant and consistent with the overall corporate strategy.

Thus, managing organizational performance must relate to achieving targets that guarantee survival today while preparing for the growth challenges of tomorrow. People within the organization must achieve high levels of performance now to keep the business moving ahead, but at the same time, individual capability must be increased to successfully handle the demands and requirements for success in the future. It is a continuous process of learning, leading, and relating.

What Successful Companies Do

Anticipation is one of the key ingredients to sustain business success—constantly looking ahead and anticipating the next steps. While this sounds like a reasonable activity, it does not come naturally to most business leaders. However, the common practice—not the best practice—is circumstances dictating behavior rather than behavior dictating circumstances. It is a matter of taking what you *get* rather than getting what you *want*. The unfortunate situation I see so often is business leaders who really are not leaders but participants—the circumstances lead, and the businesspeople participate by playing the hand that is dealt rather than starting a new game.

It is important to lay the foundation for the planning process with a situation analysis to know where you are starting from. Following are the elements of a solid situation analysis:

Values
Start a plan by knowing who you are. The values that drive the business determine all that follows. Making decisions without knowing your values could contribute to a lot of static or, lack of clarity, in the direction of the business. Business values identified as the basis for all decisions often include the following:

- Integrity
- Dignity of the individual
- Serving the customer
- Fairness in all dealings
- Teamwork
- Empowerment
- Excellence in all we do
- Superior financial performance

Maintaining and modeling specific values of the business is what creates a strong performance culture. Thus, when you start the strategic planning process with a clear understanding of corporate values, you lay the foundation for effective results.

Swot
The senior management team must know the current condition of the enterprise if it is to map out an effective direction. Performing a **Swot** analysis—identifying **S**trengths, **W**eaknesses, **O**pportunities and **T**hreats—is a good way to analyze the current business situation. Data from this analysis helps determine how to strategically deploy resources to achieve the corporate mission.

Distinctives
Another important element of knowing your current situation is to consider your strategic uniqueness, strength, or advantage. What makes your organization different? What is your niche? What is unique about your company? Then, play to your strength. Differentiation in the marketplace is an integral part of your strategy for building your business.

Market Analysis
An understanding of the market forces you face is essential for a realistic strategic plan. The market forces create the major contraints that affect your ability to sell your products or services and make a resonable profit. Pay particular attention to barriors and opportunities, both internal and

external. This intelligence enables you to plan how you will counter competitive pressures or avoid uncompetitive environments.

The behaviors of successful companies, on the other hand, present an encouraging picture. Here is an overview of the strategic planning process that can increase the predictability for success:

Strategic Planning Process—Overview

1. Conduct a situation analysis to determine what special conditions should be factored into the planning process.

2. Vision is understood and shared. It is not just a neat slogan but a well-thought-out picture of where the company wants to go—what it wants to be.

3. A mission is developed to understand what the behaviors of the company should look like to achieve and maintain a successful business life.

4. Objectives establish critical direction and enable the channeling of activity to achieve successful outcomes.

5. Strategy is understood, developed, shared, and executed to assure the resources of the company are effectively directed to optimize performance and results.

6. Plans and projects specify the activity necessary to achieve a goal, enabling the business to execute its strategies.

To make sure this process is healthy and dynamic, a champion has to make sure the business stays the course with its navigation system. The champion is critical to keep the discipline and common-sense elements in proper perspective. The process "cascades" from the Situation Analysis to the projects that implement the plan. Here is a brief graphical depiction of the process:

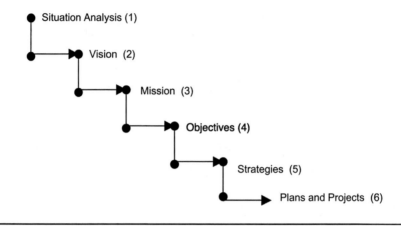

Strategic Planning Process
Strategy Development and Execution Links

- Situation Analysis (1)
- Vision (2)
- Mission (3)
- Objectives (4)
- Strategies (5)
- Plans and Projects (6)

A company following this process is writing its script for success-ful results. Many companies write the script but fail to follow through to achieve the targeted results. *Fortune* magazine reported recently that less than ten percent of strategies effectively formu-lated are effectively executed. The key to strategic planning is strategic execution. This requires management discipline, leader-ship, and commitment. It is centered in know-how.

Implementation!
Many good strategic plans have died at the starting gate. The cause of death? Not adding feet and legs to them—implementation. You must create a process to bring the plan to life. This requires more than just management; it takes comprehensive, dynamic, and disci-plined management.

A tremendous lack of knowledge abounds in the work environment in understanding how to develop and execute strategy. The businesses I have helped generally have seriously underachieved in this area. To address this serious shortfall I developed a script and a process for developing strategy and implementing it with predictable success. What I developed was not original. It is a collaboration of the ideas and practices of many teachers. But it has worked. My colleagues and I continue to work on making it better for our clients. Our request of our clients is to make it theirs. We encourage them to take from it what works and continue to improve on it.

Recently I received a call from a potential new client, looking for someone to conduct a weekend retreat on strategic planning. It was in preparation for their annual strategic planning project. We worked out the arrangements for me to provide the workshop, and I went to work learning something about my client's business. I asked to see the last strategic plan. The CEO walked over to his bookshelf and retrieved a binder that contained their last plan. It was about two years old. I thumbed through it and saw it had the basic elements in it. Some solid know-how was involved in its preparation.

Then I asked the CEO to describe the implementation process. He paused. "Well, we distributed it to all the business units," he said. That was it. Guess how much of the plan had been implemented? Not much I discovered. There was no implementation strategy, nor execution. The process was incomplete. The business was robbed of an opportunity to improve its performance as a result of a lack of knowledge and understanding how to get the most out of the whole strategic planning process.

What I just described is not unusual.

Implementation Planning

Effective implementation does not happen by "distributing the plan." It takes a lot of management. Collaboration among the management team is essential to prepare an effective implementation or work plan. For example, a common corporate goal in many companies is superior profitability, which usually is accompanied by a percentage or dollar target. Cost reduction is one strategy to achieve this. All departments in the organization will have tasks that support this strategy. This requires a coordinated effort, usually the job of the champion.

Commonly, each department, and its subdivisions, depending on the size of the enterprise, prepare work plan worksheets, which is a listing of projects with milestones and accomplishment target dates. While the concept may be common, each company will have its own special process. Each business must take the concept and make it work for them. There is no "works for everyone" approach. However, the fundamental principle of the implementation/work plan is applicable for every business. It's a universal principle. Unfortunately for some businesses, it hasn't been a universal practice. The following "think points" are offered to show how important this segment of the overall strategic planning and implementation process is:

- *Vision*—Only 5% of the total work force understands the strategy.
- *Management*—85% of most executive teams spend less than one hour/month on strategy.
- *Resources*—60% of organizations don't link budgets to strategy.
- *People*—Only 25% of all managers have incentives linked to strategy.
- *Execution*—9 out of 10 companies fail to execute strategy.

Balanced Scorecard Collaborative, Inc., *Strategy-Focused Organizations*

Implementation Tracking

As one of my former colleagues used to say, "You have to <u>inspect</u> what you <u>expect</u>." All good management systems have a feedback mechanism to ensure preferred results are being achieved. A systematic progress review of the work plan is crucial; it is a dynamic process. Some tasks will need to be redefined as more information becomes available. These are merely course corrections, similar to an aircraft making adjustments for strong winds. You know where you want to go, but you may have to factor in a new direction based on real-life feedback. Most businesses do. The key is to have a process that does that for you—and does it well.

For critical tasks, frequent review sessions are crucial. The more significant the impact, the closer the scrutiny should be. The champion must rally the right people to make sure the decisions needed to maintain momentum progress in a timely manner. Success waits for no one, but failure is patient. Be vigilant. Success comes to those who are prepared for it.

Mentoring The Future You Want

It should be no surprise that developing a quality strategic planning process requires preparation. The process we have found most effective involves these elements:

- Education—First, the right knowledge is required. Make sure each member of the team is well informed. Everyone needs to do his or her homework. It's difficult to participate and collaborate when the knowledge tank is dangerously low. This part of the process ensures everyone is well prepared at the outset.

- Application—After everyone has the basic knowledge required, conduct a work session on what a good planning and implementation process looks like. This exercise draws significantly from the knowledge created in the prior step.

- Implementation—Break out in small groups and perform small scale implementation tasks to develop familiarity with the process. This cements the focus on cooperation, collaboration, and commitment to achieve the same goals.

This process succeeds in preparing a business that is serious about creating a quality strategic planning and implementation system. The education, application, and implementation process is the cornerstone for each of the performance drivers identified as the six areas of championship performance.

Getting Started—Education

Do not assume that everyone involved in your strategic planning process has the requisite knowledge to fully contribute. The first step is to get the right knowledge in the hands of the participants. Then decisions can be made based on knowledge and understanding of the requirements to do a professional job.

Make sure of your commitment and know who is in charge. The process needs a champion to drive it. Then, establish the goal. Ask yourself, "How important is this?" "Why are we doing this?" and, "What else can I do?"

Too many organizations do an incomplete job on this critical process just from not having the right knowledge. Here is an outline of the process I use to work with CEOs to produce cogent, intelligent, and practical results.

Implementation Checklist

1. Obtain business information based on the best practices in strategic planning and implementation. See sources in the *For Further Reading—Mentoring Material* section at the end of the chapters eight, nine and ten.

2. Since the executive staff will determine the success of this endeavor in most organizations, they should be the group to go through the process, with the CEO as the champion.

3. Get the knowledge documents in the hands of the participants with the agreement that all will read them and be prepared to meet to discuss their application and why they are important.

4. The leader sets a time that the team can come together and give the subject matter their very best attention. This part of the process often benefits significantly by having a facilitator lead the group through the material with the objective of agreeing what works best for this particular organization. This is the crucial step of gaining acceptance. If your team does not get it, then the process is doomed. The CEO needs to make sure he or she gains understanding and acceptance right here or the results suffer badly.

5. Develop a schematic or outline of how the process will work, with measurable milestones. Identify and discuss weaknesses and opportunities to improve. Get comments of support and commitment. If the group is not ready, get them ready. This process should not be optional; it's what successful businesses do. Make this process the best you can make it.

6. Identify the review process for reprioritization. Rarely does the initial plan get fully implemented. The unexpected happens. Count on it. You need a process to evaluate alternatives and determine the new direction within the context of the strategic plan, addressing how other activities may be impacted.

7. Evaluate the Keys and Processes for Making Change Happen (chapter 6) and develop an implementation/management plan for launch. The management plan should identify the implementation steps for executing the strategic plan, what we call the "work plan." This is where most businesses fail. Most strategic plans end up on the shelf. Be sure to address how your plan is going to get implemented.

8. Build in regular performance review sessions to determine if the plan is achieving what you want. Look for early warning signs using key indicators such as missed due dates. Developing valuable performance indicators is a project in itself with high payback.

9. Review and approve a launch plan (or a re-launch plan). Be sure to get commitment from each participant.

Essentially this is the navigation system that gets a business where it wants to go. The better the process, the better the results.

Application

One of the elements of our Strategic Planning and Implementation Workshops includes considering the worst thing that could happen to your business. The unexpected will occur, no matter how prepared you are. Count on it. In one of my workshops, the client team came up with two situations that they considered dire. The assign-

"NO, I DON'T WANT TO STOP FOR DIRECTIONS! I'LL KNOW THE RIGHT ROAD WHEN I SEE IT!"

ment then was to develop at least three off-set strategies for each dire situation. The objective was to get them thinking, "What if it really happened? What would we do?" About four months later, one of the dire situations occurred. Fortunately, they had thought about it and had a place to start.

One of the most valuable disciplines in business is to plan for what you want, anticipating—anticipating what can possibly go wrong, and then preparing a plan to overcome any problems. Lack of anticipation normally results in poor plan execution. Successful companies are prepared to respond quickly to the unexpected. "What else can we do?" is the performance mantra.

The material presented in this chapter was not designed to provide the ultimate system. The purpose is to challenge you and your team to get in the game of developing the best strategic planning and implementation process for your business and to show you what the process could look like. The rewards are enormous.

Mentoring Questions

The following questions are offered as material for mentoring sessions. Essentially these questions provide a guide to answering the question "What else can we do?" I encourage you to think of ways to improve on this list and would be delighted to receive your thoughts (see page 198 for contact information).

1. Values
   - What values are driving the enterprise?
   - Are they understood and shared?
   - Who is on value patrol to see if you are walking your talk?
   - Are you consistently manifesting your values to your customers?

2. Current Strengths and Weaknesses
   - What do you think they are?
   - How do you stack up with your competition?
   - Are you leading with your strengths?
   - Are you strategic in the use of your strengths?
   - What are your weaknesses?
   - How are they currently affecting you?
   - What is your strategy?

3. Future Opportunities and Threats
   - How effective are you in watching the horizon?

- What is the worst thing that could happen to your business?
- How would you respond?
- How are you exploiting your successes?
- What are your current opportunities? What are your opportunities within the next three years?
- What is your strategy?

4. Balanced Work Plan Implementation
   - First, do you have a champion who is driving and monitoring this system?
   - Do the intervals for checking progress make sense?
   - What is the process for reprioritization in the event the plan needs to be modified?
   - Do you have perspective—are you getting where you want to be?
   - What is the most significant concern you have about this system supporting you to get you where you want to be?

5. Meaningful Status Reports
   - Are they timely?
   - Does the report adequately summarize where you are in accomplishing your plan?
   - Can it help participants prepare to ask good questions before attending a review meeting?
   - Are key performance indicators (KPIs) used effectively?
   - Would it be constructive to identify corrective actions?

6. Balanced Focus on Business Imperatives
   - Financial, Customer, Systems, Quality, and HR
   - What is your weakest performance area?
   - What can you do to upgrade performance and results?
   - Who is responsible?
   - How can you help them?

7. HR Development Plan with Specific Skill and
    Knowledge Targets
    - Have you identified the core competencies that you
      need to drive performance?
    - What knowledge-building initiatives are in place?
    - Do you have a plan to increase the right kind of
      knowledge that will advance your business
      performance?
    - How are you minding your intellectual capital
      assets?
    - Are your colleagues motivated to grow their
      knowledge?
    - How are you supporting them?
    - Where do you stand with employee satisfaction and
      loyalty?

8. New Product Development
    - Do you have adequate resources?
    - What is the schedule for introduction?
    - What market segments will it serve?
    - What market demands will it meet?
    - Are you competitive?
    - What are the greatest risks?
    - How do you mitigate them?
    - How can you improve your odds for success?

9. Budget and Planning Integration
    - How are the implementation/work plan and budget
      integrated?
    - Can people see that you are funding the highest and
      best result activities?
    - How are you exploiting your successes? Are you
      feeding the winners?
    - Are your strategies working?

While this list is not exhaustive, it does provide a starting point of the areas to examine for the development of a comprehensive strategic plan.

For Further Reading—Mentoring Material

William Dauphinais, Grady Means and Colin Price, *Wisdom of the CEO* (New York: John Wiley & Sons, 2000).

Terence Jackson, *Measuring Management Performance* (London: Nichols/GP Publishing, 1991).

Robert Kaplan and David Norton, *The Strategy-Focused Organization* (Boston: Harvard Business, 2001).

Robert Kaplan and David Norton, *The Balanced Scorecard* (Boston: Harvard Business, 1996).

Henry Mintzberg and James Quinn, *The Strategy Process— Concepts, Contexts and Cases, 3rd ed.* (New York: Prentice-Hall, 1996).

Noel Tichy and Stratford Sherman, *Control Your Destiny or Someone Else Will* (New York: Currency—Doubleday, 1993).

Chapter 9
Strategic Financial Management

"Only excellence earns a profit"
—Peter Drucker

- Linking Strategy and Financial Management
- Objectives of Strategic Financial Management
- Exploiting Success
- Fianancial Tools and Best Practices
- Mentoring Exceptional Financial Results
- Three Bottom Lines
- Application
- Impact of Knowledge Shortfall
- Mentoring Questions

Linking Strategy and Financial Management

Unfortunately, in too many evolving businesses, financial management has not come of age. Managers are still making too many financial and business decisions based on looking in the rearview mirror rather than taking advantage of financial analysis supported by strategic thinking.

Many good financial tools are available that can be instrumental in helping a business achieve or surpass its financial goals. Just as unconscious incompetence (simply not knowing what one does not know but should know) has impacted general management, the same is true of financial management. A lot of good and valuable financial management knowledge is lying dormant outside the doors of needy businesses. Following are some of the best financial practices to increase the predictability of a company's financial success.

Objectives of Strategic Financial Management

Business managers are accountable for the success of their enterprise. It is their responsibility to provide proper direction for their associates who are carrying out the day-to-day responsibilities. The essence of management is predictability. The better the management processes, the more predictable the results. The same is true of financial management. A strategically focused financial management process supports achieving the results sought.

A strategically focused process is one that has been scrubbed, tweaked, and modified to focus financial performance on the activities that will produce the results targeted in the business's strategic plan. The budget and financial reporting must be in sync with the strategic plan. If this is not the case in your business, you may be making significant expenditures for the wrong goods and services while missing real profit opportunities.

Exploiting Success

Problems cannot be ignored because they don't just go away. Serious problems deserve serious attention. However, the truly successful business will focus on opportunities, not problems. Enterprises that succeed in the long run make sure that opportunities are sought, identified, and resourced. Exploiting opportunities is symptomatic of a business that is alive and looking for ways to reinvent itself. Making this process a part of the business culture is a key ingredient for continued success. This thinking should drive the strategic financial management process.

Why is a process important when considering financial management? The word "process" refers to something with component parts that interact and work together in an interdependent way to accomplish a specific end. You cannot leave out a part of the system and get the best results. You should be working toward making a difference. You need financial information that can enable the enterprise to evaluate and predict financial outcomes. That requires a finely tuned process.

Ultimately, we all are judged by the results we produce. In business, the marketplace is the judge, and it's becoming more demanding and less forgiving.

Therefore, the focus becomes performance. Are you doing all you can do? Is every member of the team working at peak performance? Are all of your systems and procedures in top form? Are you making decisions based on the right data? Are you thinking about the worst competitive event that could happen? What is your contingency plan? Many managers assume all is well until a very unwelcome wake-up call arrives.

In line with the performance emphasis, you need to look at how you create and execute a budget to support the performance needed to achieve the strategic plan. The traditional line-item budget does not support that need. While it meets basic accountability requirements, a greater emphasis should be placed on allocation of funds to high-priority projects. The budget process needs to be modified to place emphasis on what performance the money buys. Specific projects are identified and expenditures are tracked by project.

Consider the financial management practices of companies who are perpetuating successful financial results:

- Employ knowledgeable, trained, and effective financial managers
- Use effective information and systems to support decision-making
- Effectively link the budget, strategic plan, and implementation plan
- Focus on balancing profitability, cash flow, and return on investment (profit and loss statement, cashflow statement, and balance sheet)

Activity-based management is a discipline that deserves serious attention, particularly in manufacturing businesses. Essentially, it is a process of identifying the value chain (hierarchy of value-producing activities) to enable the allocation of resources to the key activities contributing to profits. Budgeting should be used to allocate and track funds to these important profit-producing activities. Included, of course, is the ability to cost each process and production phase to accurately (within good business practice) determine cost of goods.

Recently, I was conducting a workshop for a CEO and his executive staff of a light manufacturing business in the communications technology sector. We were working our way through our *Critical Knowledge Summaries* and, this particular afternoon, were working on activity-based management. The participants, according to our normal practices, had read the material beforehand and came prepared to consider what they now could do to improve their operations based on this knowledge. The vice president of manufacturing, Greg, was particularly stimulated. Based on his new knowledge gleaned from the reading assignment, he had realized he did not have the financial information he needed to accurately cost several of his key manufacturing processes. This, in fact, made his cost of goods highly suspect.

The discussion among the participants that followed that afternoon was a major breakthrough for the business. The team was finally working together to get to the core costing issues that had crossed departmental lines and had remained gross estimates. This was our fifth workshop together and the team was learning to work together, where previously each department created its information as if it's a separate business. While knowledge is very important, the ability to work together as a team to apply the knowledge is a significant ingredient. Both are necessary.

In the past few years, we have worked with several manufacturing clients who had no accurate measure of their cost of goods or what products proportionately were contributing to revenue. The problems stemmed from both a lack of critical knowledge and a seeming inability for a team to collaborate and address core business issues that crossed departmental lines.

In each case, we were called in as the crisis peaked. The one common element these companies shared was the entrepreneur-founder had left the business unexpectedly. In three of the businesses, the founders had exited (death and illness) prior to adequately anticipating what vacuums they would leave if they were out of the business. Business perpetuation strategies were not addressed.

The founders of one of these businesses had an uncommon grasp of the economics of their manufacturing business, having started and operated the businesses successfully for decades. However, with increasing pressures from competitors the margins had been shrinking in recent years. After the entrepreneurs were gone, no one had filled the void they left in managing the margins. A keen focus on margins and continuously looking for ways of improving them produce preferred results. That's what the successful companies do.

The importance of continuous, vigilant evaluation of the business operations is vital. Successful companies continuously look for ways to bolster performance and protect themselves from future threats. Most importantly, they identify future opportunities that support business longevity. They have the ability to reinvent themselves, which requires knowledge. The best possible strategy is to develop the capabilities of the work force so the number of people anticipating the various ways to make the business stronger is optimized. Hence, building knowledge and challenging thinking is a remarkably efficient and effective investment in the future value of the business.

Financial Tools and Best Practices

A very good friend and business associate, Jim Horan of One Page Planning Company, has helped scores of businesses with a program he developed called *The Four Disciplines of Profit*. We have expanded Jim's program and call it *The Six Disciplines of Profit*. The program includes these elements:

1. Strategic Plan—We have covered this vital process in chapter eight, but it bears repeating. The strategic plan and its implementation make the greatest contribution when integrated with the financial objectives of the business. Each plan or project needs to be evaluated and monitored in terms of its financial contribution.

2. Budget—By definition the budget is the financial plan. Yet so many businesses run the budget process separately from the strategic plan; they must be integrated for optimum effect. Tying the budget and the strategic plan together, both in the development and the implementation stages, supports the priority that resources be aimed at those segments of the business that afford you the greatest probability for sustained profitability.

3. Income Statement—The company financials traditionally have been reserved for the very top executives in privately held companies. However, that is beginning to change. Opening the books has been found to have great impact in getting the company sensitized to the right issues. If you want your employees to feel and act like stakeholders, you have to treat them like owners. The benefits of involving the work force in the economics of the business, managed wisely, have huge upside potential. A terrific account of this strategy is found in Jack Stack's book, *The Great Game of Business*. I highly recommend reading it.

4. The Balance Sheet—This tool traditionally provides a picture of the enterprise's financial health. It shows the financial categories that you should focus on to build value. It behooves you to have a particular member of our management team assigned to each line on the balance sheet to assure your organization concentrates on optimizing your performance so the business achieves the desired financial results. Make sure your management efforts are orchestrated with a balance of knowing the financial pressure points on which to place an emphasis. This adds wisdom and intelligence to corporate direction.

5. Cash-Flow Statement—A positive bottom line certainly is a valid goal. But the one statement you really don't want to do without is this one. Even profitability is no guarantee of success. Many businesses have gone out of business while still showing a profit. They simply ran out of cash! You need to know where the cash is coming from, where it is going, what your future needs are, and how they will be met. Cash is the blood-flow of the business and deserves close scrutiny and management.

6. Financial Model—This tool enables you to regularly evaluate the "what ifs" in regards to optional programs and processes. You can evaluate likely outcomes and answer the question, "Is this particular change going to create the results we are looking for?" This is a most valuable tool in anticipating the preferable direction to take. All too often the finance department just provides a look at history. You need forward-looking analysis to enable you to make better resource decisions.

Having these useful tools in place is just the beginning. Too often this valuable information gets produced, distributed to a limited audience, and then gets filed. It's almost a spectator's sport in some businesses. Smart business managers are using this information to get in the game and perpetuate success.

Yes, there is a lot of information to contend with. But the key information can be gleaned and presented in such a way that the drudgery is removed and the important lead indicators are tracked, so you can focus on taking the right steps. Management has the opportunity to make the use of key financial information a team sport. You should make it a big deal because it is.

Mentoring Exceptional Financial Results

Starting on a simplified basis makes a lot of sense. In implementing change, keep the process simple and manageable. Every business is different. Shortcuts to implementing a strategic financial management process do not exist nor should they. The management team should spend quality time developing a process of managing the enterprise that they can commit to—understanding that the very survival of their business is at stake.

Three Bottom Lines

In their very practical book, *Managing by the Numbers*, authors Chuck Kremer, Ron Rizzuto and John Case present a valuable concept on tracking three bottom lines. This is based on the fact that a well-run business has three important financial statements and that each has its own important bottom line. Usually the focus is on profits. But that can be deceiving. It is one element of successful financial performance—but it is only one. It does not tell all you really need to know to be sure you are on the right track to financial success. The three bottom lines are

- Net Profit
- Operating Cash Flow (OCF)
- Return on Assets (ROA)

Net Profit—This number comes from the income statement, and shows whether your company's revenue for any given time period exceeds its costs. It shows whether you are making money or not. As a performance measure, it has value. But it has drawbacks in that it can mask valuable information about cash and managing your fixed assets. You need more information to give you the best picture.

Operating Cash Flow (OCF)—This comes from the cash-flow statement. It shows you how much net cash is flowing into your company, independent of what you may receive from investors and lenders and independent of what you spend on fixed assets and other investments. It shows the cash you are generating from your business operations. In general, OCF should consistently be larger than net profit. This is an indication that the business is doing a good job of managing assets such as receivables and inventory.

Return on Assets (ROA)—This is calculated by dividing net profit by average assets. It also gives you feedback on how effective you are at managing your receivables, inventory, and fixed assets. And, it is a widely used indicator for comparing your performance to competitors in the same industry.

Financial Scoreboard ($000)			
			Days: 365
Beginning Balance Sheet 12/31/00	*Income Statement*	*Cash Statement*	*Ending Balance Sheet* 12/31/01
Cash 25		Cash Change -5	Cash 20
Accounts Receivable 0	Sales 500	Collections (OCF) 470	Accounts Receivable 30
Inventory 75	Cost of Goods Sold 350	Inventory Paid (OCF) 380	Inventory 105
Other Operating Assets 0		Prepayments (OCF) 0	Other Operating Assets 0
Notes Receivable - Trade 0		Lend (Receive) (OCF) 0	Notes Receivable - Trade 0
Gross Fixed Assets 100		Fixed Asset Investment (ICF) 0	Gross Fixed Assets 100
Accumulated Depreciation 0	Depreciation + Amortization 10		Accumulated Depreciation 10
Net Fixed Assets 100			*Net Fixed Assets* 90
Other Investments 15	Intangible Amortization 1	Other Investment (ICF) 0	Other Investments 14
Total Assets 215			*Total Assets* 259
Accounts Payable 0	MSG&A Expense 155	Expense Paid (OCF) 105	Accounts Payable 50
Debt 10		Borrow (Payback) (FCF) 11	Debt 21
Other Operating Liabilities 0	Interest & Other Expenses 1	Interest & Other Paid (OCF) 1	Other Operating Liabilities 0
Income Tax Due 0	Income Tax Expense 0	Income Tax Paid (OCF) 0	Income Tax Due 0
Nonoperating Liabilities 0	Nonoperating Expense 0	Nonoperating Exp Paid (FCF) 0	Nonoperating Liabilities 0
Stock 205		Paid In (FCF) 0	Stock 205
Retained Earnings 0	>>>Net Profit -17	Dividend & Other (FCF) 0	Retained Earnings -17
Total Liabilities + Equity 215			*Total Liabilities + Equity* 259
	>>>Return on Assets -7.17%	>>>Operating Cash Flow -16	

The better you make these three bottom lines, the better you make your business. From a financial perspective, improvement on the three bottom lines is the goal of a business.

Next, you should consider how you get this perspective into a financial scorecard. A very good tool developed by Lou Mobley brings this all together very nicely. Mobley taught in the IBM Executive School over a twenty-seven year period beginning in 1956. His specialty was simplifying complex financial reports into an understandable form for non-financial executives. In doing so, he created the "Mobley Matrix" or what is now called "The Financial Scoreboard." Take a look at the process of making the really relevant financial data flow through the three bottom line reports (see Financial Scoreboard, above). I should add that one of the authors, Chuck Kremer, has a wonderful seminar on financial business literacy. Kremer's book, *Managing by the Numbers,* is a must for your executives.

"I CONVINCED THE BOARD THAT BREAKEVEN WAS A GREAT YEAR."

Application

Surprisingly, breaking even in some settings is accepted as a reasonable result. Granted, it is tough to create a profit year after year. As Peter Drucker said in his book, *Managing for Results*, "Only excellence earns a profit." One of our clients recently commented to her fellow board members that if you are not getting at least 8% return on investment, you should have your funds in a low-risk portfolio, where you can at least do that without the risk. The reason one takes risk is to exceed the 8%.

Our experience in helping clients find ways to increase profits starts with a situation analysis that usually discloses unconscious incompetence. They did not have the critical knowledge of what to do to create profit improvement. The range of knowledge shortfalls usually is not too broad. The most common include not knowing costs and not spotting deteriorating trends quickly enough.

Another situation that we find is a company accepting less than stellar financial performance too long before doing something about it. It's as if they are hoping "performance will get better if we just keep doing what we are doing." That is indicative of not having enough knowledge or experience in the old knowledge data base to confront the negative forces of business. It usually starts appearing first in the financial performance.

One of my colleagues has a specialty consulting practice that focuses on financial management training. One of his workshops is on financial management for CEOs. One of his exercises is to have the class construct the main categories of their P&L down to net income. The next step is to assume they have just experienced a 10% reduction in sales/revenue. Then they are asked to identify their options for getting back to profitability. My colleague commented that this exercise is really an eye opener for most of his CEO class members.

First, most of the CEOs have a tough time constructing a P&L statement. Second, a 10% revenue loss is usually pretty devastating for those who can construct their P&L, and generally they don't have ready answers of what to do next. The value in this experience is taking the group from this situation (where the CEOs realize they have a real knowledge gap) to an "aha" they take away, intent on getting more familiar with the financial management of their business.

Impact of Knowledge Shortfall

Then there's the situation where the financial staff does not have the knowledge or experience to spot a developing problem. One of my early CEO appointments resulted from the need to bring in new leadership to address seriously deteriorating financial performance. I did my due diligence on the company prior to accepting the position, making sure I was not jumping into an impossible assignment. In this case, my evaluation involved meetings with all the executives who reported to the CEO, the auditors and legal counsel, as well as key board members. After I became satisfied that the job was doable, I put my employment deal together with the board and moved in.

The business effectiveness of this enterprise started with the CEO and the executive staff—my direct reports who ran, in this case, the six operating departments—that enabled the company to achieve its business objectives. I had a general sense of what I was going to do to get the team capabilities at the level needed to deliver the required business performance. However, before implementing my plan, I needed to spend time with the staff and confirm my initial assessment.

Assessing the performance capabilities of the executive staff is a crucial first step in developing a performance improvement plan. It's the key internal process. The key external process involved developing an understanding of the market, our position in that market, how our products and services fare in the competition for more business, and the like. Essentially, I performed an internal and external SWOT (strengths, weaknesses, opportunities, and threats) analysis.

Eventually, I replaced two of the department heads. The skills needed to get this company on a speedy path to recovery and then building new business success required skills that two of the staff just could not produce. I feel bad about having to impact people's lives with a major career interruption. However, I have learned two important facts. Number one, I owe the company, its shareholders, and employees the very best performance we can post. To do less is unacceptable. Therefore, I must do all I can to have performers on the team who can contribute to creating the best possible business results. I will do all I can to help them catch up but there is a point where a person's performance shortfall and business demands just don't allow it. Second, a termination/replacement can be accomplished with dignity and respect. It may be painful, but it can be fair and just. I do it as I would want it done to me.

Of the two, the really difficult one was Ed, the chief financial officer. Ed was disabled which exacerbated the whole process. He was a wonderful, thoughtful person. He was just in way over his head. This company had experienced tremendous growth—revenue tripled in the last two years. It had been growing about 50 to 70% per year the prior three years. There was no budget. I asked for a budget and Ed didn't know where to start. Financial statements were available 45-50 days after the close of the month. It got worse.

Ed had been hired nine years earlier as a full-charge bookkeeper. Subsequently, as the company grew rapidly over the past seven years, he was promoted to senior accountant, finance manager, controller, and vice president of finance and chief financial officer. It was unfair to everyone, but I see it happening all the time. Further, the people Ed had hired over the past several years were underprepared. We had a very weak finance department. I foresaw it weeks earlier and had started the recruitment process actually before Ed left. This was a perfect example of the Law of Diminishing Expertise that I described in chapter one. Fortunately I was able to hire a top CFO who developed a great crew of motivated financial professionals. They played a key role in the financial turnaround and subsequent growth.

In companies that are achieving predictably solid financial performance, skilled financial analysts spot a negative trend, and the performance commandos are called to get involved and figure out how to turn the trend. In too many companies, the financial data is still in the old accounting mode of looking in the rear view mirror to see how performance was weeks and weeks ago. To be successful in the ever-increasing competitive game of business, you have to have strong awareness and an astute financial process to help guide and monitor performance. They are a crucial part of the success process.

Mentoring Questions

Here are some worthy mentoring questions we suggest you evaluate for the highest payback on effort to impact your financial performance.

1. Managing by the Numbers
   - Do you share the financials with your managers? Do they understand your financial situation?
   - Are the managers trained to understand and manage financial performance?
   - Are managers being held accountable for financial results?
   - Are incentives tied in with financial performance?
   - Are your managers thinking like owners?

2. Focused, Concise Financial Reporting
   - Are your financial reports providing information that helps create future direction?
   - Are they a part of the managers' tool kit and can they use them effectively?
   - Can you identify and rank profit contributors?
   - Can you identify and rank cost contributors?
   - Do you have a quarterly review to see what successes can be exploited?

3. Broad-based Financial Participation
   - Do you have a financial scoreboard that keeps everyone focused on the critical numbers?
   - Does your financial scoreboard reflect the business performance at a glance?
   - Is everyone in the game?

4. Use of Key Performance Indicators (KPIs) to Track and Lead Performance
   - Can you measure your work output in key performance areas?
   - Do your managers use KPIs to track and manage performance?

- How valid are they? Do they have a positive impact on performance?
- Do you have lead indicators that provide an early warning about possible problems?
- Are you comparing your performance to industry standards?
- Do you have an initiative to improve KPIs?

5. Visible Cash Management System
   - Is your cash management systematized to the point you feel confident you have needed cash through the fiscal year?
   - How is cash management integrated with budget and performance reporting?
   - How can receivables be managed as well as costs?
   - How can inventory be managed as well as costs?
   - Do you have a strategy for building cash reserves?
   - Do you have underused assets on your balance sheet that could be converted to cash?

6. Budget as a Management Tool
   - Do you have broad-based participation in the budget process?
   - Are funds being allocated to the highest-profit-producing activities?
   - Are budget allocations tied to performance?
   - How often do you have budget performance reviews?
   - Are incentives tied to budget performance?

7. Financial Modeling
   - Do you use a financial model to evaluate alternative financial choices?
   - Can your financial model help you predict budgetary threats or opportunities early enough to respond proactively?

For Further Reading—Mentoring Material

Robert Bacal, *Performance Management* (New York: McGraw-Hill, 1999).

James Brimson and John Antos, *Activity-Based Budgeting* (New York: John Wiley & Sons, 1999).

Chuck Kremer, Ron Rizzuto and John Case, *Managing By The Numbers* (Cambridge: Perseus Publishing and Inc. Magazine, 2000).

Lawrence Serven, *Value Planning* (New York: John Wiley & Sons, 1998).

Jack Stack, *The Great Game of Business* (New York: Doubleday, 1992).

Chapter 10

The Systematic Practice of Management

"Things which matter most must never be at the mercy of things which matter least."
—Goethe

- The Practice of Management
- Purpose of Management
- The Prepared Manager-Leader
- Managing Corporate Performance
- Mentoring Systematic Management
- Application
- Mentoring Questions

The Practice of Management

The American business environment, or culture is in a dramatic process of change. The way businesses manage themselves, compared to even ten years ago, is quite different. Some business managers still cling to the old ways, but they are limiting their careers and the businesses they run. Companies that cling to the way it used to be will have a short future. Take a look at differences between the old culture and the new culture:

<u>Old Corporate Culture</u>	<u>New Corporate Culture</u>
• *Being a manager*	• *Being a leader*
• *Being a boss*	• *Being a coach and mentor*
• *Controlling people*	• *Empowering people*

- *Having a central authority*   • *Distributing leadership*
- *Being competitive*   • *Encouraging collaboration*

A new management leadership style is required to transition from the old to the new culture. An open mind and looking for more effective means to achieve preferred results must drive the leadership style. Tomorrow's competitive edge will belong to those who successfully develop and execute a strategy to deal with these changes.

What is driving this change? Knowledge! Twenty years ago, Peter Drucker predicted that the workforce was becoming predominately knowledge workers. At the turn of the new century the workforce is approximately 80% knowledge workers. They are more highly educated not only in dealing with more developed levels of technology in business but knowledge of interpersonal strategies and techniques to drive business performance. The workplace is behaving differently. Here's what knowledge workers expect:

Knowledge Worker Expectations

- To be respected and treated with dignity, not treated as a commodity

- To follow sound leadership, not be managed

- To be mentored and coached, not abandoned

- To be guided, not directed

- To be empowered to make a contribution, not limited through control processes

- To participate in decision-making, not have decisions constantly coming from the corner office or from corporate

- To be involved in collaboration with colleagues, not in competition

---

The professional managers who are succeeding have spotted these trends and learned how to be effective leaders rather than bosses. Bosses are becoming scarce, particularly in companies that are the high achievers. Bosses don't always know how to bring out the best performance in their human resources. The most highly valued skills in managers today are relationship skills. That's what it takes to get the best out of your human resources. And this is your most valuable asset and your highest cost. To underachieve here is deadly expensive.

Purpose of Management

Unfortunately, some managers have erroneously interpreted the best way to lead knowledge workers is through laissez-faire management—let everybody do their thing and we'll pull it together at the end of the month' hopefully. I was taken aback on several occasions during visits to some of the high-tech companies during the highly euphoric period that followed funding. The key performance indicator (KPI) was bodies hired. There was no management strategy, nor discipline. This was the new economy. Well, the rest of the story is now known. It was wrong and became the "tech wreck." Fundamental business management theory and practices had been abandoned.

How did it happen? Too many very bright techies and specialists did not have the knowledge nor experience of how to successfully run a business. It was technology driven, not managed. Many costly lessons have been learned again. Sustained success is no accident. It is the result of a well-thought-through strategy with competent execution. The desired results are identified, and the resources mobilized and managed according to a plan to deliver the desired outcomes. That is the purpose of management—deliver the desired results with a high degree of predictability.

The Prepared Manager-Leader

First, let's look at the environment most managers are now facing. I am including all levels of managers, from the CEO down.

- A very smart workforce that has a low tolerance for nonsense—they want to play to win.

- Competition that is on an international scale—it's a world market now.

- Change that is daunting and is still picking up speed.

- Customers who are committed to find the best quality for the best price. No sloppiness here.

And here's what is needed to succeed—preparation, preparation, and preparation. How many people do you know who are in management positions who have not been trained as managers? You probably know many. The old problem of promoting a great performer into a manager of performers is still happening. Sometimes it works, but rarely does it deliver the optimum or preferred outcomes. This is one area where change is not happening fast enough.

Olympic athletes are among the most focused individuals you will find when it comes to preparation. On average an athlete preparing for an Olympic event will spend 1,200 days in preparation, just for a few moments to perform for the gold, silver, or bronze. But they do it because they know that is what it takes. To be a successful manager today requires being an effective leader of knowledge workers. Here are a few characteristics of today's effective manager-leader:

- Solid understanding of the management and leadership processes required to be effective in a business setting

- Knows most of the important business practices and how to use them

- Has developed relationship skills to enable strong followership when needed

- Is committed to continuous learning and growth—models and mentors it

The more you prepare, not only does the likelihood of your success increase, the more prepared you will be to serve your colleagues as a mentor and teacher. More and more, each manager-leader has a responsibility to oversee the knowledge development of those for whom he or she has responsibility to lead.

Managing Corporate Performance

Positive economic performance is management's reason for being—its single most important purpose, the one activity that will enable its continued existence. The business can justify its existence and its authority only by the financial results it creates. A business enterprise fails if it is not successful in

- Producing positive financial results

- Supplying goods and services desired by the customer

- Maintaining or improving renewal capabilities to sustain positive financial results

Recently, Robert Kaplan and David Norton, in their book *The Balanced Scorecard*, introduced a keen approach that brings together several dimensions of strategic management and measurement in improving corporate performance. They have received broad acclaim for articulating a practical approach that combines strategy, management, and measurement. In particular, this recognition has come from numerous successful businesses transitioning into the next century with focus, energy, and commitment.

Kaplan and Norton used the analogy of running a successful business to sitting in the cockpit of a powerful jet aircraft. A pilot relies on important indicators to get his or her aircraft and its valuable cargo to the desired destination. Similarly, today's CEO and senior management need the right navigation system and performance gauges to assure they get where they want to go. This is a good example of systematic management.

The balanced scorecard provides the executive team and corporate managers with the instruments they need to navigate their corporation to desired results. It is a framework we can use to turn our vision, strategic plan, and work plan into a scorecard that provides feedback on the effectiveness of our tasks and projects. The scorecard should let us know if our efforts toward championship performance are really getting the results we want without having to track and sort through a myriad of details.

The balanced scorecard retains an emphasis on financial performance but also addresses precisely what drives the company's financial results. The scorecard introduced by Kaplan and Norton measures organizational performance across four balanced perspectives:

1. Financial
2. Customer
3. Internal systems and quality
4. Human resources growth and development

The perspective gained from a well-designed scorecard lets you focus on activities having the greatest impact on overall performance. Too often the executive team has to sort through too many performance indicators to translate information into a meaningful conclusion. A well-designed scorecard can enhance communication, understanding, and management attention to achieve breakthrough performance for customers and shareholders.

  1. Financial Perspective—These measures indicate whether a company's strategies, implementation, and execution are contributing to bottom-line improvement. These are the most familiar measures, and they are used most often since the success and perpetuation of the business are determined in large part by these measures and results.

2. <u>Customer Perspective</u>—The customer is the business. To know if our business is on the right track, we must have some feedback on how we are doing with our customers. That would cover how effective we are at getting new customers as well as retaining them. Too often, significant resources are devoted to bringing in new customers without looking at the cost/income implications of low-customer retention. This has broad operating implications that impact the health of the business significantly. We need to expand our knowledge and respond smartly to this important area.

3. <u>Internal Systems and Quality Perspective</u>—Here we need to identify the critical internal processes or systems in which the business must excel. As stated earlier, the definition of management is predictability. In large measure, that predictability is determined by the quality of the internal processes. These processes allow the business to deliver the quality product/service needed to meet the wants of the customer and meet shareholder expectations of financial results.

The measures used in this perspective need to address not only the existing processes but also the innovation that will be needed to continue to satisfy the above requirements. You have to be thinking of improving the present while designing and measuring the future.

4. <u>Human Resources Growth and Development Perspective</u>
The fourth perspective involves identifying the infrastructure the organization must build to create long-term growth and development. This is where most companies currently are in trouble. They are not preparing their employees to meet the increasing demands of change. The customer and internal processes perspective should identify the factors most critical for current and future success. The business will be unprepared to address those factors, however, unless the learning and growth issues are in balance. The

emphasis here needs to be on people, systems, and organizational procedures.

Developing a reporting mechanism around these perspectives, such as the scorecard, also significantly contributes to defining focus for the executive team. Executives tend to build their careers within a single function. Accordingly, they are often biased toward their functional specialty.

These biases can lead to blind spots, especially in companies where departmental barriers (walls) have been allowed to develop. Blind spots are areas of relative ignorance and it is difficult to form teams and create consensus around them. This most often occurs when there is little shared understanding about overall business objectives and how the various functional units can integrate and contribute to those objectives. Adapting a scorecard-type management system can be a significant catalyst for consensus and teamwork.

Because the executive team develops the scorecard, it helps build a team focus and shared model of the entire business to which each member has contributed. The scorecard objectives then become the joint accountability of the executive team. Consensus and teamwork builds among the members as they execute their responsibilities. Further, the scorecard creates a common language to communicate information about how the company is doing to all business associates. Since most people in an organization want and need to know the score, it helps build consensus and commitment at all levels.

Kaplan and Norton deserve a lot of credit for developing this system of evaluating corporate performance. However, I would like to suggest that you consider a slight modification that adds two more perspectives for evaluating performance. And, this takes us back to chapter four where the six performance areas for championship performance are identified. As you review them, see how they correspond to the Kaplan and Norton perspectives:

• Strategic Planning and Implementation

- Financial Management
- Systematic Management
- Leadership
- Performance Relationships
- Learning and Growth

In my workshop for strategic planning and implementation, I have now turned the four perspectives into these six high-performance strategies.

Mentoring Systematic Management

To achieve success in these critical areas, management must be focused on the performance areas that create the predictability for success. Under any scenario, business success is becoming a struggle, but management can take steps that will increase the likelihood of success. The six strategic areas just identified can be used in the mentoring process to strengthen business performance. In establishing a mentoring agenda for each performance area, again, consider:

Education—build knowledge about why it is important
Application—build knowledge about what it looks like in
          use
Implementation—build knowledge about how to put it to
          work

Within each of the four to six scorecard perspectives, I recommend identifying the systems involved in delivering the services to its customers, inside and outside. A system is defined as *an organized group of related activities that together create a result of value to customers* (Drucker). To achieve high performance, you must know what processes are contributing then focus on making them the best you can. Measurement should be part of the systematic feedback to track improvements. You have to measure what you want to manage. Measurement identifies potential actions, which is what we are looking for in our quest for high performance—"What can we improve?" Measurement should take us there. I recommend Michael Hammer's book, *The Agenda,* for an excellent discussion on the relationship between systems improvement and performance measures.

Before leaving the topic of measurement, consider one concept—that two levels of measurement exist in a business. The two levels are

- Corporate performance
- The actions to improve corporate performance

First, corporate performance measures comprise the corporate guidance information. These measures let you know if you are on course. Included in this category are the typical financial measures, inventory level, turns, ratios, and so on.

The next level of measurement, actions to improve corporate performance, should provide feedback on improvement initiatives. For example, if you want to reduce customer returns, you identify the main cause for returns, establish a project to fix the problem, and then measure your progress to make sure you achieve the goal.

Application

"WELL, THE FENG SHUI DIDN'T WORK WOODRUFF. NOW WHAT?"

The search for solutions can take you down some unusual paths. Many executives belong to tech groups or roundtable discussion groups, which can be valuable experiences. However, sometimes problems get dealt with superficially. One of my CEO friends often returns from his tech group meeting seemingly ready to try whatever was discussed that month. His executive staff groans, "Oh, no, not another flavor." Yes, it happens in many different ways. Leaders looking for solutions sometimes create some very interesting initiatives.

How do you build knowledge that will provide clarity for improvement opportunities? One approach that has worked is to get the people together who have an impact on performance. (Yes, almost everyone does; so trim the participants to the most logical and workable gathering.) Use some book, paper, or film to introduce knowledge targeted at improving performance in some manner. Have everyone read the material then come together prepared to ask, "Is there something in the material we read that we can use to improve our performance?" Have someone who can get people involved in dialogue facilitate the process. I have used this process for over twenty years and it is amazing to see what can be created. Give it a try. You will be delighted with the results.

How do you sort out the practical management processes from the fads—particularly when the management fads have some very compelling attributes? My advice is to review these five basic questions when evaluating any process.

Test the Process

1. What are the true costs of implementation and subsequent maintenance?

2. What benefits will be realized, short and long term?

3. What are the risks and can they be mitigated?

4. How will the culture deal with the change?

5. Does this process have longevity? What will it look like
    in five years?

The flip side of this coin is to take a look at what the really successful businesses are doing. That brings us back to the best businesses practices. Our observations, based on evaluating successful business practices, is that changes to the management process are studied and evaluated by a team of leaders prior to any changes—a management impact analysis. Knowledge is the key commodity and knowledge management is crucial to continued success.

One of my colleagues has a company that specializes in estate planning. He asked if I would assist one of his clients with our executive team development program. The company was about twenty years old, involved in light manufacturing in the high-tech optical sector. As a first step, we usually conduct certain diagnostics to make sure our training and intervention are in sync with what the client needs, believing that prescription without diagnosis is malpractice.

Our assessment is designed to identify performance shortfalls so we can assist the client immediately in addressing these improvement opportunities. In this case, the shortfalls were so serious we never really got to the intervention and training. Executive team training would have fallen into the same category of a responsive rescue measure as rearranging the deck furniture on the *Titanic*.

It was probably the worst case I have seen of a manufacturing entity not having any semblance of quality processes, including documented systems and improvement initiatives. How had they survived this long? In the early stages of the business, they enjoyed almost no competition, based on technology they developed. As others saw the business opportunity, superior technology was developed by a larger, well-financed company. The response to this competitive challenge was an attempt to increase the sophistication and performance of two core products—but with limited manufac-turing-engineering know-how. Customer returns were mounting, as were losses. It turned out to be a turn-around engagement and sale of the business.

This was another ugly business story. What distresses me is the fact so many businesses plod along, with their knowledge base under-developed, trying to compete in an environment where the knowl-edge complexity is advancing. Astute business leaders need to be asking, "What knowledge do I need to have on board to be suc-cessful in this market?" We are finding most business problems are knowledge based. Most companies don't have a strong understand-ing of what knowledge they should be developing for current oper-ations, much less what knowledge they will need over the next two to three years just to stay competitive. The situation is alarming.

What is the state of your knowledge management? The answer will tell you a lot about your preparedness for creating and perpetuating success for your business.

Mentoring Questions
Following are a few improvement categories and related questions to get you started.

1. Producing Positive Financial Results
The first task of management is to evaluate every act, every deci-sion, and every deliberation in terms of economic impact. Here are a few topics to consider for building knowledge and discussing application.

- How do you build company value?
- What are the elements of a quality financial system that provides the essential analytical information to guide performance?
- What is the general financial understanding of the immediate senior managers guiding corporate perform-ance?

- How is your feedback process working to keep people abreast of how your company is doing?
- How do you evaluate competing demands for funding— cost benefit analysis for everyday use?
- How do you identify and support the most profitable activities?
- Are you using the budget as a management tool?
- What are your applications of financial modeling?
- Do your managers have a working understanding of the basic accounting/financial reports: balance sheet, P&L statement, and cash flow statement.

2. Internal Systems and Quality

The quality of the business's systems plays a very significant role in developing predictability in the business results. The essence of management is producing predictable outcomes. Well-managed systems are an essential element.

- What is the status of your identification and evaluation of systems?
- Do you know the hierarchy of systems contributing to business results?
- How effective are you at systems process mapping? How do you develop an understanding of what a system does?
- Have you appointed one champion per system—some one responsible for the well being of the system?
- What are your system improvement initiatives? Do you keep looking for ways to make systems better?
- How is your systems documentation?
- Is quality a part of your business culture?

3. Strengthening Customer Emphasis

The customer is the business. Building a cultural awareness and discipline regarding customer care is vital and requires vigilant cultural reinforcement. Great insights can be obtained from studying companies that are following these principles. The books listed at the end of this chapter can provide material for this purpose.

- What does great customer care look like?
- What is the best approach for a company like yours? Does everyone understand and consent to this approach?
- How would valuing the internal customer—treating the next person in the process as a customer—help you?
- How do you keep your customer care sensitivity at all levels? Does everyone understand how important it is? Is management setting an example?
- What can you do proactively to build solid customer relations?

4. Getting the Most from Your HR Assets

The responsibility of corporate management is to make a productive enterprise out of human and material resources. The company cannot be a mechanical assemblage of its various components. It must be an effective whole—better than the sum of the parts. What's your strategy? It is clear that human resources are the only resources capable of enlarging and enhancing a business's performance. Developing highly successful people at all levels has the potential to create greatness.

- Are you perpetuating the knowledge and practices of what great managers do? (Most managers are thrown into the deep end with little preparation. This is one of the biggest and best areas for immediate benefit for improving business results.)
- Can you identify the optimal knowledge your managers should have today and what they should be working on for a successful tomorrow?
- What is the core knowledge that creates most of the value in your company? What is your strategy for growing it?
- If knowledge is the weapon of the future how are you preparing for battle?
- What strategy should your company use to provide incentives for the development of critical knowledge?

Too few CEOs have taken on the role of the chief knowledge officer. But consider this—most companies are now made up of knowledge workers. The leader of the knowledge workers is the CEO. CEOs have a significant opportunity to put a greater emphasis on knowledge growth and its application to the business. Imagine the CEO as the white knight leading the battle against unconscious incompetence. Does it work? Take a look at what Jack Welch did at GE.

For Further Reading—Mentoring Material

James Collins, *Good to Great* (New York: HarperBusiness, 2001).

James Collins and Jerry Porras, *Built to Last* (New York: HarperBusiness, 1994)..

Peter Drucker, *Managing for Results* (New York: Harper & Row, 1964).

Peter Drucker, *Managing for the Future* (New York: Truman Talley, 1992).

Michael Hammer, *The Agenda: What Every Business Must Do to Dominate the Decade* (New York: Crown Business, 2001).

Linda A. Hill, *Becoming A Manager* (Boston: Harvard Business, 1993).

William Pollard, *The Soul of the Firm* (Grand Rapids: Zondervan, 1996).

Chapter 11
Leadership At All Levels

"The price of greatness is responsibility."
—Winston Churchill

- Perspective on Leadership
- Leadership Characteristics
- The Changing Leadership Model
- Mentoring Leadership
- Application
- Mentoring Questions

Perspective on Leadership

Exercising the right kind of leadership at the appropriate time makes a difference to the outcome of an endeavor—whether it is the running of a multinational company, organizing a new product launch, directing the annual community charitable drive, or arranging a retirement dinner. Organizations endowed with people who exercise creative resourcefulness develop followership along the way. This kind of leadership can be developed throughout the organization, and it enables a business to produce exceptional results.

Most leadership occurs without any awareness that it is happening. You'll find an opportunity for leadership in almost any role—manager, husband, wife, father, mother, and others. The extent to which you create the best possible results is dependent on how well you fulfill those leadership roles.

The more you understand what leadership is and how to develop and deploy it in your business, the more prepared you will be to meet the challenges you face in an increasingly competitive business environment. Through leadership development, businesses can be prepared better to achieve higher levels of success. This will require a specific strategy.

The future of business rests in the hand of its leadership. That's not so profound. What is profound is the fact that the fastest growing businesses today utilize shared leadership—decentralized, broad-based leadership. Recent studies (see sources at the end of this chapter) have revealed that in successful organizations, certain patterns of leadership are being repeated—every leader works and every worker leads. The new term "workleader" is rapidly being popularized in the business environment.

This trend reflects a growing reliance on empowerment and participation in the business processes—with leadership occurring at all levels. Where is this leadership coming from? Essentially, it is being developed from within: homegrown leadership. Workers at all levels are filling leadership vacuums created by the downsizing of mid-management structures. Teams are also becoming more integral in work processing by providing self-management direction. A new era for leadership has arrived, and prepared, committed individuals will heed the call.

Leadership must be developed at three levels—individual, team, and organizational. A strategic development process will ultimately enable employees to contribute to the business mission more comprehensively.

How can one provide effective leadership without understanding what it is? The distinction between *managers* who *do things right* and *leaders* who *do the right things* is attributed to authors Peter Drucker and Warren Bennis. The successful enterprise has learned to embrace and merge both roles: leader-managers who can identify the right things to do and then do them right.

As you examine leadership, it helps to have a definition that includes more than just what leaders do, but also *what* they create and *how* they create it. Leaders see opportunities to create results, and they seize them. They ask, "What else can I do?" They proactively look for ways to achieve exceptional performance. These features need to be considered when it comes to what is being mentored or coached. Taking these factors into account, consider this definition of leadership:

> *Leadership occurs when individuals anticipate and identify an opportunity to make something positive happen, and then take responsibility for the process and its results.*

Leadership Characteristics

What does great leadership look like? Let's go back and review the example from chapter two about building greatness in an organization. I included the following diagram to highlight what is required to build a culture in which great leadership incubates and thrives. Consider the question, "Does the leader create great events or do the events create the great leader?" In a business context, it is most often revealed that the great leader creates great results. And one of the significant accomplishments of a great leader in today's business environment is to create a culture in which leadership is cultivated, modeled, and mentored.

Using Abraham Maslow's hierarchy of human needs, business cultures that produce superior performance support behaviors that enable people to self-actualize—feel great and be motivated about contributing at their highest level.

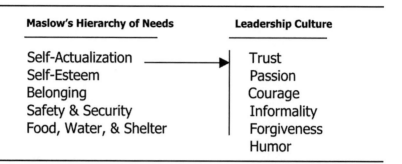

Maslow's Hierarchy of Needs	Leadership Culture
Self-Actualization	Trust
Self-Esteem	Passion
Belonging	Courage
Safety & Security	Informality
Food, Water, & Shelter	Forgiveness
	Humor

Creating the leadership-friendly culture is no accident. The characteristics the CEO must demonstrate set the tone. What a huge opportunity and responsibility! Creating a culture that unleashes the best possible behaviors of the troops is what builds greatness in business operations and results. People are motivated to give their best. That is leadership. Here are some of the leadership characteristics we have found in organizations' cultures that are moving toward greatness.

Leadership Characteristics of Great Companies

- Trust

Leadership starts with trust. Followership does not exist without trust. It is foundational. If you fail to create this foundation, your leadership is going to be extremely limited. Leaders have recovered after fracturing trust, but it is rare and difficult. My advice is to do everything you possibly can to engender trust and then defend it with all your ability. The troops can forgive just about any blunder as long as they trust you.

- Passion

Modeling passion and rewarding passion supports the attainment of greatness. Have you ever studied a person who is truly passionate about what they are doing? Compare that person with someone who just shows up, does his or her job, and is out the door as soon as he or she can escape. Cultivating a culture that rewards exceptional performance supports the development of the drive to achieve excellence that I would describe as passion. Be sure you have identified leaders in your organization capable of being passionate about what they are doing. That usually accompanies other qualities that contribute very well to corporate objectives.

- Courage

One of the more difficult aspects of leadership is to do what is right when it is not pleasant or easy. For example, some leaders suffer from wanting to be popular or liked. They postpone or avoid the difficult calls. Most often this is manifested in not taking action on problem personnel counseling or terminations when they are needed. Great leaders make the hard calls that may even be unpopular. Great leaders know how to make the hard calls and have the courage to follow through. This attribute separates the good from the great. Lack of courage to make the tough calls has lowered many an organization to mediocrity.

- Informality

In today's business environment, formality just creates another barrier. Astute leaders have discovered ways to balance informality and openness to support better communication and relationship skills. Formality contributes to bureaucracy, which tends to stifle innovation. Since innovation drives achievement, it makes sense to diminish a threat to innovation—formality. Balanced informality is what leaders need to model so the troops know what it looks like. It's not just dressing down and not wearing socks. Informality means reducing barriers to open and meaningful dialogue about business excellence.

- Forgiveness

Have you ever worked in an organization where if you made a mistake it dealt a serious blow to your career? It's awful. This kind of organization creates a risk-averse culture with people avoiding taking any significant break-through chances. Any major business advancement requires risk. Risk management is what good leaders use. If a leader makes a mistake and gets the corporate death sentence, innovation ceases. Leaders have to be able to make mistakes—then fix them just a quickly as possible. Forgiveness drives innovation. Balance is what makes this process work.

• Humor

Leaders can't take themselves too serious—if they do, others won't. Being able to laugh at oneself and encourage a sense of humor about business is good business. It supports the kind of attitude that makes the business process more enjoyable and gets more people involved in the fun of making a business successful. People want to be successful. It is more pleasant and rewarding working in an environment where we can see the humorous side of success. Innovation surfaces more often when people are enjoying their work. Humor reinforces enjoyment.

The Changing Leadership Model

James Belasco and Ralph Stayer, in their book, *Flight of the Buffalo*, provide us with a terrific model of what is happening in many successful organizations regarding leadership. The old leadership model is likened to the head buffalo that grandly led the herd.

Buffalo are loyal followers of one leader. But the astute buffalo hunters learned the surefire way to increase their success in collecting buffalo hides was to shoot the lead buffalo. The rest of the herd stood around, waiting for the leader to show them what to do next. It was deadly for the poor buffalo, just as it is for many employees when the leadership model in their organization isn't working, for whatever reason. Depending on just one leader is no longer an option for an action-oriented business that is driving for success in our highly competitive marketplace.

A new, more successful model is likened to a flock of geese. If you watch a flock of geese flying in their "V" formation, you can't help but notice the lead position in the formation is frequently changing. Every goose is responsible for getting itself to wherever the gaggle is headed, changing roles whenever necessary, alternating as leader or follower.

What a terrific model. Imagine the power unleashed in your organization when the doers alternate between leading and following to create the right mix to reach the desired destination. It has daunting implications on an organization's performance. The more I see of this model in aggressive, get-it-done companies, the more I'm convinced this is the preferred way to build shareholder value while creating sustained performance capability. Let's now take a look at another form of shared leadership.

In our business culture in the past decade many CEOs have become celebrities. America, and the press, delight in creating celebrity status even for its business leaders. Some of the more recent shining lights are Lee Iacocca at Chrysler, Jack Welch at GE, followed by a spate of new technology personalities—Bezos, Case, Dell, Jobs, Gates, Grove, Ellison, and McNeely. But a look behind the scenes reveals there is a lot of co-leadership contributing to the success these stars represent. Warren Bennis, a professor of business administration at University of Southern California and David Heenan co-author of, *Co-Leaders: The Power of Great Partnerships*, just completed a five-year study of co-leadership primarily in the executive setting. Bennis commented in an interview that successful co-leadership in an organization can be achieved in three ways:

- *Fast Trackers*—These are the people who are on their way up the ladder and understand they must have achievement, loyalty, and perhaps a few breaks. They are adept at building consensus and followership and understand the value of sharing power.

• _Back Trackers_—These are former senior-level executives who have downshifted. They often distance themselves from the hard-driving, deal-making arena, shunning the limelight and the related pressure. They are more comfortable with quiet power, staying in the background.

• _On Trackers_—Either they do not want the top spot or it is never offered to them. They are comfortable remaining on a top-notch team. Bennis says for the co-leadership format to work, someone has to park his or her ego outside the executive office door. This is not always an easy task for a lot of driven, hard-charging, do-it-now types. But this type of leadership style often runs out of gas as the demands of the fast-changing business environment mount. Partnering and collaboration is unleashing more creativity in the executive office. For the longer term, this step eliminates fewer people and allows more leaders to participate.

In the past few years, I have seen more and more of this approach used in growing businesses or in turn-around situations. Since the designated leader may not have all of the needed qualities or skills, a shared-chairmanship or office of the chairman comprised of a small, powerful team, often is called on to fill the too-big shoes needed for the immediate business challenge. Usually, bright and committed leaders can find a way to share power for the common good when the situation demands it. Those who can't may be passing up the best solution. It can work, but the big competitive ego usually won't fit.

The research findings of Jim Collins and his colleagues in his latest book, _Good to Great,_ emphasized this. He studied the leadership style of the CEOs of eleven companies that triumphed over time and sustained long-term great performance. He calls the leadership style of these CEOs "Level 5" leaders.

"Level 5 leaders channel their ego needs away from themselves and into the larger goal of building a great company. It's not that Level 5 leaders have no ego or self-interest. Indeed, they are incredibly ambitious—*but their ambition is first and foremost for the institution, not themselves.*"

Following are the levels and types of leadership Collins identifies.

Level 5 Hierarchy

Level 5   **Level 5 Executive**
Builds enduring greatness through paradoxical blend of personal humility and professional will.

Level 4   **Effective Leader**
Catalyzes commitment to and vigorous pursuit of a clear and compelling vision, stimulating higher performance standards.

Level 3   **Competent Manager**
Organizes people and resources toward the effective and efficient pursuit of predetermined objectives.

Level 2   **Contributing Team Member**
Contributes individual capabilities to the achievement of group objectives and works effectively with others in a group setting.

Level 1   **Highly Capable Individual**
Makes productive contributions through talent, knowledge, skills, and good work habits.

Mentoring Leadership

When everything is in sync among leaders in the organization, it's like observing a world champion sports team in its best form. Even when Michael Jordan was the star Chicago Bull in that team's heyday, he deferred to his teammates when it came time to make a basket. He did what it took to get the ball through the hoop, whether that meant he or another player made the shot. The objective was to win and use the cumulative talent to do it. Michael scored a lot of points, but four other players assisted in the process, making it possible. Championship players understand the importance of optimizing the use of talent to win. And it is spilling over more and more into the business arena.

The once popular image of the CEO was that of an all-powerful titan surrounded by a pack of gofers. In the early days, who knew of anyone at Ford Motor Company other than Henry Ford? It often takes a very strong leader to establish momentum in a business, and at times it is invaluable. But more and more businesses are discovering they don't need a star personality who often silences co-leaders who dare to dissent or compete for the spotlight. The best thinking is needed—no matter where it comes from. But for this to happen, the culture must be supportive. What does that kind of culture look like? How does it happen? Let's look at some of the strategies that encourage power sharing, partnering, and co-leading.

- *Celebrate the Enterprise, Not the Celebrity*
Some of the best-run companies in the United States (for example, McDonalds, Wal-Mart, Westinghouse, Xerox, and General Motors) are directed by all but invisible leaders and co-leaders. The people who run these businesses rarely appear in the personality magazines or have their homes shown in *Architectural Digest*. People in these businesses make a difference collectively. The team is the focus, not one player.

- *Cultivate Egalitarianism*
Eliminate the caste system. Elitism is an expensive luxury that doesn't work anymore. Modest executive offices are to be found more and more in thriving businesses. Reserved parking spaces, exclusive dining rooms—all the trappings of power and elitism—ought to be reduced to facilities for everyone, sending the message, "We're all in this together." More business leaders are recognizing success is often 70% culture and 30% technology.

• *Foster Togetherness*

Common vision galvanizes unified performance. Successful organizations avoid people who drain all the energy out of the organization without giving anything back. As leaders, you want to cultivate energy. A common vision is a big contributor. Teamwork is being recognized more and more by business leaders to be the preferred vehicle to drive championship performance. Leveraging talent is more attainable in an environment where each player is motivated to rise to the occasion, making his or her best contribution.

• *Strengthen Self*

A healthy dose of self-confidence prepares one to step back and follow or step up and lead. Knowing this and doing this is critical. It's not a case of "I gotta win every time!" Some people seem driven to lead the conversation, establish the agenda, or top the last story. This translates to insecurity, and insecure people do not make good co-leaders. Managing oneself to be a catalyst for results instead of seeking prominence can unleash even greater results in the knowledge-worker environment. It does take healthy, enlightened self-management.

• *Nurture Trust*

Trust is crucial in a participative environment. It is as important as vision and common sense. Relationships of trust don't just happen. They evolve, having been proven time after time based on multiple, predictable, or expected outcomes. Trust tends to flourish in environments where thought is given to the importance of the work at hand on a collaborative basis. Quality relationships are developed by quality leaders.

• *Purvey Hope*

Confucius said, "A leader must be a dealer in hope." True, a leader sees the opportunity and the obstacles, but he or she has confidence that the obstacles will be overcome and the opportunity will be realized. In galvanizing enthusiasm and commitment to achieve a common goal, a leader, regardless of where he or she sits on the organizational chart, helps create hope for better outcomes. Hope and optimism support application of creativity to the business processes. And that definitely increases the likelihood of success.

• *Institutionalize Dissent*

Organizations that cultivate constructive dissent have a higher probability of success than those who do not welcome the "emperor has no clothes" message. The truth, whether delivered in an unvarnished state or sensitively packaged, has to have an audience—or we risk great peril of being blindsided. Of course, in the interest of cultivating healthy, strong relationships, the sensitive delivery of a strong message augurs better overall results. Don't tell your spouse he or she has bad breath; just hand him or her the mouthwash. In the executive office, healthy dissent can be an enjoyable, creative process. Keep it as constructive as possible, and be certain to cultivate it.

• *Redefine Loyalty*

Blind loyalty has a significant downside. A loyal colleague should be able to tell you when you are wrong or even heading in the wrong direction. Leadership history is loaded with disastrous cases where loyal followers supported bad judgment and direction. Real loyalty responds as a caring counselor. Loyal colleagues should always measure what is being asked of them against their most basic values.

• *Balance Power*

The thoughtful and sensitive use of power is a hallmark of a great leader. Great leaders realize that they develop power by granting it to others. A cornerstone of shared leadership is shared power. It is a unique balance—too much and you become a figurehead, too little and you squelch creativity and commitment. Balance is usually achieved after finding the successful middle ground, which will vary based on the chemistry of the team. The balance is in there somewhere and the successful leaders find it. Just keep checking to make sure it hasn't been lost once you find it.

• *Build Team Goals*
Leaders build consensus, unity, and common direction. They understand that the greater good comes from thinking beyond oneself and encouraging orchestrated outcomes. Building buy-in is part of a consensus-building process. Making it better through broad-based involvement does not eliminate competitive ideas; it channels them positively. The contest should not be among the people but among the ideas.

Every organization is different. Each has its own cast of characters with their specific role to play. Yet there are general guidelines in the enactment of work that can provide support for higher-level outcomes. The strategies presented above could serve as a discussion outline in a team-building workshop or at your next staff meeting. I highly recommend cultivating discussions among the people sharing leadership toward answering the crucial question, "what else can we do?"

"OK, WE'RE AGREED. WE GET THE SAME 50% BONUS AS LAST YEAR. WORKFORCE GETS A 1% RAISE!"

Application

The credibility of the corporate leadership team has a significant impact on building a corporate attitude about performance. Modeling the kind of leadership you want in your business emanates from the top.

One of my clients, let's call him Robert, is a superstar in this regard. He has an uncanny ability to understand the perspective of those he leads. He knows his strengths—and weaknesses—and does not engage in handing out baloney. He's straightforward and his colleagues know they can depend on a good, honest answer. Also, if he doesn't have an answer, he'll say so and ask if any of his teammates do. They know he is the boss, but they work with him as a member of the team. He's approachable. He's consistent.

He also is a great student of what it takes to be a good leader. He works at it. His success as a leader is not accidental. It is the result of a carefully executed strategy based on knowledge and some natural abilities. Robert is committed to be the best leader he can be. He feels a huge responsibility to his team and to his business to play his position to the best of his ability, knowing he has to continually work on his skills. That is modeling leadership at a highly effective level.

Mentoring Questions

Following are some specific leadership mentoring topics to consider building a mentoring session around:

1. Leadership Competency
   - What is the leadership model in your business?
   - How do the CEO and executive staff treat the rest of the troops?
   - Is there a level playing field?
   - Are you all playing by the same rules?
   - Do you see uniform commitment and performance?
   - Is the leadership producing committed followership?

2. Management Competency
    *   What are you doing to assure that your managers
        have the basic understanding of what successful
        managers do?
    *   How do the knowledge of preferred management
        practices and effective leadership merge?
    *   If competent managers increase the likelihood for
        success, what can you do to strategically increase
        the odds for success?
    *   Who is responsible?

3. Shared Business Objectives
    *   Is your management team working with shared
        objectives?
    *   How about the rest of the company? Are you all on
        the same page, pulling together?
    *   What initiatives are in place to unify focus and
        commitment?

4. Shared Decision Making
    *   Where do most decisions get made? Top down or
        bottom up?
    *   What is the benefit of broad-based decision making?
    *   How do you prepare an organization to share/
        decentralize decision-making?
    *   What are the benefits/risks of shared decision-
        making?
    *   How do you create a culture of shared decision-
        making that succeeds?

5. Taking Responsibility for Results, Regardless of Title
    *   What are the benefits of people taking
        responsibility for results?
    *   How do you encourage people to take
        responsibility?
    *   How do you think the culture in your organization is
        dealing with mistakes/bad decisions?

- How do others in your organization think our culture is dealing with mistakes/bad decisions?

6. Meaningful Rewards
   - To what extent are you using performance-based rewards?
   - Are your incentives producing the results you want?
   - What other areas may benefit from incentives?
   - Are you adequately and fairly rewarding your high performers?

7. Performance Assessment and Feedback
   - How good are you at giving meaningful feedback?
   - What do the troops think of your methods of assessment and feedback? What could you do better?
   - What role might this area have in building your intellectual capital?
   - What would it look like if you were very proficient in this area? What results should you expect?
   - Is this a good area for investment?

8. Communication Effectiveness
   - Are you helping your colleagues develop in this area?
   - How are you doing generally? Do you have any problem areas?
   - Where could you improve?
   - What are the benefits?

9. Modeling Integrity, Respect, and Culture Values
   - Are integrity and respect priorities for senior management?
   - How is the trust level in your organization?
   - Is followership difficult or easy to create?
   - Can you think of some strategies to strengthen your overall performance in this area?

For Further Reading—Mentoring Material

Warren Bennis and Burt Nanus, *Leaders: The Strategies For Taking Charge* (New York: Harper & Row, 1985).

Warren Bennis and David Heenan, *Co-Leadership: The Power of Great Partnerships* (New York: John Wiley & Sons, 1999).

James Belasco and Ralph Stayer, *Flight of the Buffalo* (New York: Warner Books, 1993).

Jim Collins, *Good to Great: Why Some Companies Make the Leap...and Others Don't* (New York: HarperBusiness, 2001).

James Hunter, *The Servant* (Roseville, CA: Prima Publishing, 1998).

John C. Maxwell, *Developing The Leaders Around You* (Nashville: Thomas Nelson Publishers, 1995).

Emmett C. Murphy, *Leadership IQ* (New York: John Wiley & Sons, 1996).

Chapter 12
Productive Performance Relationships

"People must believe in each other, and feel that things can be done and must be done; in that way they are enormously strong. They must keep up each other's courage."
—Vincent Van Gogh

- Using Your Emotional Intelligence
- Working Together—The New Model
- Relationship Skills & Performance
- Relationship—Building Strategy
- How Do Teams Really Work?
- Mentoring Relationship Skills
- Application
- Mentoring Questions

Using Your Emotional Intelligence

Do you ever wonder why one of the most difficult tasks of senior managers is achieving consistently high performance from their people? Getting top performance is possible, but it takes a lot more than common-sense management or simply applying the latest management tool. That is because most of us, although schooled in good business, fail to understand the power of relationships. People aren't merely a component in our complicated business machine—they make up the very engine! When we fail to understand the power of this engine, no management method alone can deliver the kind of results we desire.

You can make a difference in the lives of others in and through your work environment. The difference can be for the better or for the worse. Effective relationships are no accident. Much of the responsibility for positive results depends on you. Positive relationships bind people together to enable exceptional performance. Look for individuals who possess some of the most important skills in a business environment. The ability to work together effectively is what releases potentially unused human resources. Consider the impact of having unused ability mobilized because of improved relationships.

Humanity appears to have an incredible capacity for growth. As a leader, you have a unique role for facilitating other people's developmental growth. However, it is difficult to lead someone else further than you have gone yourself. The skills and strategies discussed in this section have the potential to affect your relationships and those with whom you have the responsibility to lead. Fortunately, human-relationship skills can be developed.

Daniel Goleman first introduced the concept of Emotional Intelligence (EQ) in 1995 in his book, *Emotional Intelligence*. Goleman drew from his behavioral research as a psychologist. His research addressed how individuals with very high IQs may be ineffective in areas of leadership. In fact, IQ did not equate to relationship skills. Those of modest IQs could be very high in EQ. The good news is that EQ can be developed, unlike IQ. Emotional intelligence includes self-awareness, persistence, zeal, self-motivation, empathy, and social deftness.

With the recent emphasis on the work group, more companies now screen applicants for effective human-relation skills. The ability to work together effectively is essential in the age of the knowledge worker. People who work together effectively can facilitate the participation of all the contributors to the process. An environment less supportive of participation may limit valuable contributions.

Career success is increasingly influenced by a person's effectiveness in using relationship skills. In fact, it is one of the most valuable skills upper managers can have. One of my CEO responsibilities has been to assess relationship-building skills for the following three purposes.

First, all things being equal, I want to build an organization around people who can effectively enable a collaborative work process. It simply makes sense that more effective results emanate from work process centers with a pro-collaboration orientation than those struggling with relationship problems. Collaboration is in; confrontation and competition are out.

Second, colleagues who are less effective in using relationship skills should be focused on developing these skills. That process can range from reorientation and education to one-on-one coaching and professional counseling. The human personality is multifaceted, complex, not easily changed, and terribly exciting! A significant opportunity exists to help create an awareness of the importance of specific behaviors. If the individual can reach inside and produce these desired behaviors, the individual and the organization should be applauded.

Third, potential leaders can exist within any organization. Individuals with ideas and the passion to realize them are awaiting opportunities. If they are to lead us in the future, we need to create a climate conducive to growing their leadership ability and generating intellectual capital—ideas, innovations, learning, know-how, and strategic alliances. The responsibility to create these opportunities must be taken seriously, and once they are established, results will soon follow.

You can expect both victories and failures as you lead people to work together. Responsible stewardship requires you to try, regardless of the outcome. In many cases, you seek not to create new behavior as much as to stop annoying or unproductive behavior. Usually, this involves helping individuals see and understand their unproductive behavior and letting them know the consequences of not changing it.

Some managers seem content with simply accepting relationships as they are—apparently not trying to develop them. More often than not, these people have not pursued critical knowledge that allows them to move beyond the status quo. A huge opportunity exists for managers of this type when they choose to learn the skills necessary for developing positive relationships. The improved results they will experience significantly enhance their ability to contribute to a winning team.

Working Together—The New Model

Much has appeared in the business press during the past decade regarding the impact of social skills on career success. A manager's job is to get work accomplished through people. Having the social skills to do that effectively is essential to the job. As his or her career progresses, a manager's technical competencies become less important, while his or her social skills become increasingly important.

The social arts or the people skills are competencies that make for effectiveness in dealing with others. Deficits in these competencies lead to ineptness or repeated interpersonal problems. It is the lack of these skills that can cause even the intellectually brilliant to founder in his or her relationships. While this may not destroy the career of a manager, it certainly can impact his or her effectiveness and future career advancement. These social abilities allow one to shape and encourage a relationship and to mobilize and inspire others to work together effectively. An effective manager must have these skills.

The level of effort I see in many companies to strengthen these skills is disappointing. The old bottom line requires a lot of attention. But investing in people is equivalent to investing in the system that creates the bottom line. Neglecting one of the most important opportunities to enhance corporate capabilities and performance just doesn't make sense. It is an opportunity too often overlooked. And the effort must be a long-term one—firmly established within the culture.

Daniel Goleman discusses the elements of interpersonal intelligence (social competence) in his book, *Emotional Intelligence*:

> *In many workplaces today, talented, productive people are being thwarted or sabotaged by gaps in emotional intelligence—in themselves, their bosses, and the others around them. In many organizations, we're caught up in an atmosphere of autocratic and sometimes abusive management, mountains of rules and red tape, traumatic downsizings, and a fear-laced climate of uncertainty, perceived inequities, resentment, and anger. We show up and keep our hearts closed and our heads down, just hoping to get by and collect a paycheck. Studies have revealed that it is actually emotions that are the "essential activating energy" for ethical values—such as trust, integrity, empathy, resilience and credibility—and for social capital, which represents your ability to build and sustain trusting, profitable business relationships. At the center of these traits is something every great leader must have: the capacity to create excitement. It is this inner fire that will transform the current workplace and build great companies with teams ready to compete for the future.*

The social skills described by Goleman are apparent in the ability to organize groups, negotiate solutions, have empathy and create rapport. People who possess these skills can connect with people quite well, be astute in reading reactions and feelings, lead and organize, and handle the disputes that are bound to flare up in any human interaction. A high level of social competence is necessary to create a level of comfort, support, and enthusiasm.

These are the natural leaders, the people who can express unspoken collective sentiment and articulate it in such a way as to lead a group toward its goals. These interpersonal abilities are only one aspect of emotional intelligence. Numerous other manifestations exist, but it is primarily social competency that supports a manager's leadership. Being able to understand and identify these characteristics, or lack of them, greatly enhances the mentor's ability to more comprehensively assess mentoring strategies and direction.

Relationship Skills and Performance

One of senior management's significant responsibilities is to define the corporate vision and culture, and then model and coach them into fruition. Creating a culture that nourishes the strongest and most effective work relationships requires strategic human-resource development. Four specific skills emerge as major components of interpersonal or emotional intelligence:

1. *Organization*—Involves initiating and coordinating the efforts of an association of people. The leader directs the efforts of others to achieve predetermined objectives.

2. *Negotiation*—Involves preventing conflicts or resolving them when they do occur, usually be a mediator. People who have this ability excel in finding the common thread that will create the greatest amount of support for a particular objective or solution. This is demonstrated in diplomacy or arbitration or finding the all-important middle ground that the group can support.

3. *Empathy*—Involves connecting emotionally with other people. This facilitates getting involved in an encounter or recognizing and responding appropriately to people's feelings and concerns. Empathy is the art of relationship building that supports team performance and builds esprit de corps.

4. *Rapport*—Involves insightfulness regarding people's feelings, motives, and concerns. Sensitivity to others' feelings leads to caring relationships, a valuable trait in building followership.

Taken together, these skills represent what is seen as interpersonal intelligence. Let's look at these skills on the three human-resource levels—those of the individual, the team, and the entire organization/culture—and see how they can be developed.

Relationship-Building Strategy

Creating an awareness and appreciation at the individual employee level for the importance of positive relationship skills is a crucial beginning point. This is part culture, part learning, part leadership, and part team development—actually it is pervasive in the development of a high-performance organization. Look at world-class sports teams, as well as businesses that are creating world-class results. There are exceptions, no doubt. But in most exceptional performance situations, arguably you will find exceptionally high levels of mutual commitment among the individual participants. It is this kind of commitment that management-leaders want to examine to see if the same kind of relationships, which not only support superior performance but actually fuel it, can be replicated.

In the process of building an organization, the logical place to strengthen the impact of effective social skills is at the point of intake. Make sure the recruitment and selection process is effective in examining this attribute. No system is foolproof, but several good screening processes are available to assist in identifying strengths and potential deficiencies. Building competence in evaluating social skills produces an excellent return on investment.

Developing Individual Relationship Skills

As leaders, your most significant contribution to an individual in building his or her relationship skills is to identify the preferred behaviors—and model them. If the CEO and senior staff do not model the preferred behaviors, they do not become a part of the culture. And if the senior management team knowingly suffers unsociable behavior, that message is communicated loud and clear. The counterproductive impact on the culture is obvious in this case.

Developing relationship skills on an individual basis begins most effectively with training in order to build understanding and awareness. A well-designed training class on relationship skills is the place to start. Major benefits spring from a common experience in culture building. Going through the classes together creates community as well as common language and understanding. This is a good process to use in development wherever possible. Once a common understanding is found, it is the easier to mentor the kind of behavior you want to achieve.

Several very useful approaches help identify individual styles of interaction. Myers-Briggs, DISC, and the Hunsaker-Alesandra models are three I have used and found to be effective in establishing a common framework for identifying and working with different behavior styles. Opportunities can be created to dialogue about the different approaches to relationships and constructive interaction. This is a great tool for mentoring.

One of my business partners, Linda Williams, shared the following with me.

> "I'm a Driver Style. One thing I learned is that I don't always give people my attention. So I had a deal with my people. If they came in my office to talk to me and I kept going through papers on my desk, or whatever, they would simply say, 'I see you're in driver mode.' That snapped me out of it and I gave them my full attention. As you can guess over time I did not need this reminder. I find understanding your style and how to deal with other styles invaluable from a relationship building point of view."

Knowing your own limitations and how to compensate for them is important, particularly in the behavioral coaching arena. The models should facilitate discussion, thoughtful consideration, reflection, and then more discussion, always in a non-threatening manner. Leaders and mentors are facilitators. By building good relationships, profitable transactions will follow.

Developing Team Relationship Skills

Building relationship skills is at the core of enhancing group effectiveness. The group or team creates a relationship experience based on individuals brought together for a common cause. Since the current trend in the workplace is for people to work together in small groups or teams, it behooves managers to seek ways to increase the effectiveness of these work units.

Basic to effective group performance is mutual support and commitment. When this exists, you will have the beginning of harmony. The presence of harmony in a group is one of the enabling processes that move a group to become a team. The operation of a team has the potential to significantly increase the quality of output. Understanding how to achieve harmony in a group is a valuable skill.

The situation described above is different than conflict. Not all conflict is unhealthy. Peter Senge was quoted in *Fortune* magazine as saying:

> *In great teams, conflict becomes productive. The free flow of conflicting ideas and feelings is critical for creative thinking, for discovering new solutions no one individual would have come to on his own.*

For all its unsettling nature, discontent or disagreement can prove to be a hotbed of creative ideas and opportunities to build deepened trust and connection. Constructive, not destructive, discontent can produce major break-through thinking. This is part of the culture you are attempting to create in the relationship skills development process: an environment in which individuals take responsibility not only for results but for conditions that can change ordinary results into exceptional results. This process starts with the commitment to create positive relationships that support trust, harmony, focus, and excellence.

Developing Relationship Skills Throughout the Culture
Although a lot has been said already about the importance of modeling in establishing the culture, it is important to emphasize again that no one does it more effectively than the senior management team. They are the cultural trendsetters. This applies to just about every action every day.

How Do Teams Really Work?
Some terrible misconceptions about teams abound in the business environment. In fact, the term "team" is overused and misused. Perhaps I am overly sensitive, but at the risk of being so, calling a group a team is a disservice to all involved. Let's be clear about what a team is and what it does. At the core is how well the members work together. A group shows up at an event—be it work or recreation—and goes through the motions of working together. Members of a team quickly identify who can play which position best and how each of the players can support the others in the overall effort to achieve the highest level of performance to win the game.

I will never forget one client. When I arrived at his business office, I saw several department heads wearing company team buttons on their lapels. Yet, within the first couple of hours on the premises, I learned that two of the department heads were having a serious relationship problem, resulting in almost no communication between them. "This is a team?" I muttered to myself. Here was a serious misunderstanding about what a team is all about. Fortunately, over the next several months, the group did become a very good team. It did not just happen. It was the result of the participants seriously studying what it takes to become a great team, getting commitment from each individual, and going through the mental workouts to achieve team understanding, commitment, and then performance.

During my career, I have had the privilege of developing several very effective, enduring executive teams. I have discovered that an up-front review with the team of exactly what it takes to be a great team and what is expected of each of them to remain a member of the team is vital. It's a package of behaviors I have mentored to my colleagues to produce a championship team of executives. I have termed it "S-I-L-E-C-T Championship Team Behaviors."

SILECT Championship Team Behaviors

Support—Each member of the team must support the other members in whatever form is necessary to achieve the team goals.

Initiative—The success of the team depends on each member taking initiative for results. The good ideas need to bubble up, not be handed down.

Loyalty—Each member of the team needs to know his or her back is safe. If a problem exists, it gets resolved between the specific team members who are having the problem; the matter doesn't get subjected to third-party reviews.

Empathy—If one of us hurts, we all hurt. If one team member has a problem, then we all do. You need to understand your teammates' biggest problems and biggest opportunities. Then you can contribute.

Commitment—Commitment to the team members and the team goals needs to be modeled. A cohesive executive team does much to build confidence in the business leadership.

Trust—Trust is the glue that holds all relationships together. It's to be protected like crown jewels. Building trust in the organization is one of the significant leadership opportunities of the executive team. Trust is one of the most far-reaching attributes of the team, as well as of executive leadership.

It is unfortunate when the team function often is handed over to a group, and the group never progresses to the point of functioning as a team. A huge opportunity is missed. Once in awhile there may be an enlightened soul in the group who can rescue a situation like this. But far better results can be realized from a distinct team development strategy.

One of my most delightful team experiences occurred in one of my early experiences as a CEO. I had been recruited to rescue a dental insurance company that had incurred serious losses and was in management disarray. Actually, the business was sound, but it had grown very rapidly and had outgrown the management. Some bad underwriting decisions were allowed to be made by the marketing/sales department. Essentially, the rescue was facilitated by building a new, invigorated executive team and turning them loose to do their jobs. The star was Dr. Bruce Craswell. It helped that Bruce was very bright—he received his D.D.S. at age twenty. But Bruce was also blessed with an engaging ability to develop immense followership from everyone around him. Bruce was an astute problem solver and a delight to be around.

Bruce was one of three new department heads I recruited. The other two were the vice president of finance (CFO) and vice president of claims processing. Along with three remaining department heads (underwriting, marketing and sales, and information technology), we implemented the SILECT behaviors. But Bruce really modeled them best. He personified SILECT. He helped all his colleagues solve problems in a way that really built deep, meaningful relationships. He was gifted. The behaviors caught on and so did outstanding performance. A group of executives became a great team in about six months, and the company was back in the black in about eighteen months, going in the right direction and building good financial reserves. Bruce was a great catalyst in the process on morphing a group to a high-performance team.

Not every team-building scenario I have experienced has had a Bruce. But I have found that a bright, supportive player early in the process can help model what you want to produce. The variations on this theme have been numerous. The successes have always been assisted by the bright achievers who are looking for a way to build a more successful business. Everyone's career opportunities are enhanced in a thriving, successful business. And that is what championship teams produce.

In another business situation, I was introducing SILECT as the new CEO. I had been appointed by the board of directors after a search process and what I call the "beauty contest" where the candidates are processed through several layers of interviews. I was one of three outside candidates—there was one inside candidate. After getting the appointment, the board chairman and I had dinner with the inside candidate. We wanted to be assured "John" and I could work together and John could accept not only not getting the appointment but working for the person who did. I should add John was three years from retirement. John said he would support me as the new CEO.

A few weeks after reporting for duty and going through the SILECT ground rules for the executive team, one of the other department heads I had inherited "Carl" asked to see me. Carl was very uncomfortable and said he wanted me to know that what he was doing was for the good of the team, and he was committed to see that this team worked because there was a lot at stake. Carl shared with me that John had some resentment and he was saying he didn't believe the new guy (me) was on the "right track" and a few other non-supportive comments. It seemed John had shared this view with a couple of his fellow department heads.

I invited John to my office.

I shared with John that some of his comments regarding his view of my performance had come back to me. He looked surprised but did not deny his comments. I told him I could understand his disappointment in not getting the CEO position, however, there were some absolutes involved in remaining in his position. First, if he had a problem with anything I was doing, he needed to discuss it with me. No one else could do anything about it, so no useful purpose was served by reviewing his concerns about me with anyone but me. Second, I told him the ground rules for the executive team (SILECT) were absolutes. He could not stay in his position if he did not embrace them wholeheartedly. Third, if I ever heard a similar comment, he would be dismissed. And finally, I told him he was welcome to stay if he could give me and the job his full support and commitment. John did have a good reputation for positive business results and I knew he could be a good contributor if he could get over his disappointment and think more clearly.

It all worked out well. During that time we developed a good team with only one executive position turnover—one I had to initiate. All in all, SILECT works.

Mentoring Relationship Skills

Let's reconsider a term introduced earlier—"workleader." What you want to develop in your organization, in order to truly see it empowered, are workleaders. Workleaders are the colleagues who will be involved in continuous learning, leading with knowledge and enhanced by their social intelligence. That is your model: workleaders modeling top achievement in learning, leading, and relating—individually, in teams, and throughout the organization.

The workleaders aren't just the CEO and the department heads. They exist at every level and contribute to the total effort. Your strategy on a day-to-day basis is to maintain that kind of momentum.

Application

Relationship skills create the conduit through which meaningful communication can flow. The better the relationship, the bigger the conduit. Skilled leaders understand this phenomenon and work hard to assure that they build positive relationships with those with whom they work. It's just smart business. And it has become one of the most sought after skills for key executives—you have to have it to build followership.

"IF I WANTED FEEDBACK, M°DONALD, I'D CALL MY WIFE!"

About three years ago, I received a call from a CEO who had recently bought out his partner in their business. He was now running the business, which was a nice size service company that had been in business over fifty years. His problem was that his executive team was not functioning very well. Two of his department heads were not speaking to each other. Generally, there was a lack of understanding of how teams work and how each member of the team has a position to play to assure that the team was effective and successful. An added element was that the company had recently installed an employee stock ownership plan, so people were aware that "if the company does well, we all can do well." The CEO asked me to facilitate a team-building process.

The opportunity was to add knowledge to this executive group (not a team) to build understanding and support for the importance of working together for the common good. Several members of the group did not understand how their attitudes and behaviors were affecting performance. For six months, we worked together on how to build a high-performance team, one that could produce championship performance. In that time we had a major breakthrough. My two worst offenders in the relationship problem not only got the message but also took responsibility to become significant contributors in building a team that really looked out for each other's welfare. They discovered the value in making sure they were contributing as much to their teammates' success as their own. They began treating each other as customers ("How may I help you?"). The group became a real team. About a year after the engagement, I received a call from the CEO telling me they had just completed their best quarter—ever! He was very excited. Yes, relationship skills do play a significant role in unleashing a team's best efforts.

Mentoring Questions

Here are a few questions to help build a better understanding of what well-developed relationship skills can contribute to your enterprise.

1. Harmony
   - What does harmony add to the communication-cooperation process?
   - What do you think the impact is on an organization when a lack of harmony at the top exists?
   - What are some of the techniques to build harmony?

2. Trust
   - What are the main contributors to trust?
   - Is there a good business reason to encourage and build trust in an enterprise?
   - How does trust affect leadership and followership?
   - How is your culture doing in this regard?
   - How can you build more trust?

3. Morale
   - What are the main contributors to morale?
   - What are the main detractors?
   - How are you doing?
   - Can you think of any ideas to improve morale?

4. Collaboration
   - Why would some people not want to collaborate?
   - What are the benefits of collaboration?
   - What areas are you not collaborating in that you would benefit from doing so?
   - What are some of the collaboration skills?

5. Camaraderie
   - Is this a good thing?
   - What does it contribute?
   - What is the difference between harmony and camaraderie?
   - What steps would you take to increase camaraderie?
   - What are the risks of too much?

6. Mutual Support and Commitment
   - Why is this important?
   - What can it accomplish?
   - What should your position be related to our culture?
   - How do you model?
   - How do you demonstrate mutual support and commitment to new hires?

7. Constructive dissent
   - Do you have any problems with aggressive dissent?
   - Do you want any dissent, constructive or otherwise?
   - How should you manage dissent to keep the situation from getting worse? How can you make it constructive?
   - What does a culture that allows dissent say?

8. Aggressive Helpfulness
   - What if you treated everyone in your company like they were customers? What would that create?
   - In what ways would it be good for the business?
   - In what ways would it be good for the people working in the business?
   - How would you start such an initiative?

- Would it work if only one unit or division did so?

9. Healthy Customer/Outside Relationships
    - Have you checked in lately to see how much your customers love you?
    - What is it they like most? What do they like least?
    - If you don't know, here's an opportunity!
    - Is it easier/more beneficial to get new customers or keep the ones you have?
    - What's your strategy?
    - Who is involved?
    - Is it working?

For Further Reading—Mentoring Material

Robert K. Cooper and Ayman Sawaf, *Executive EQ* (New York: Grosset/Putnam, 1997).

Aubrey C. Daniels, *Bringing Out the Best in People* (New York: McGraw-Hill, Inc., 1994).

Daniel Goleman, *Emotional Intelligence, Why it can matter more than IQ* (New York: Bantam Books, 1995).

Stephen C. Lundin, Ph.D., Harry Paul, and John Christensen, *Fish: A Remarkable Way to Boost Morale and Improve Results* (New York: Hyperion, 2000).

Jeanne Segal, *Raising Your Emotional Intelligence* (New York: Henry Holt and Company Inc., 1997).

P.M. Senge as quoted by B. Dumaine, "Mr. Learning Organization," *Fortune*, (October 17, 1994, 147-157.)

Chapter 13
Learning and Growth

"The only things that gives an organization a competitive edge— the only things that is sustainable— is what it knows, how it uses what it knows, and how fast it can know something new."
—Laurence Pyusak
The Knowledge Advantage

- Self-Leadership and Development
- Taking Responsibility
- Knowledge as a Resource
- A Learning Organization
- Knowledge Management
- Mentoring Continuous Learning
- Application
- Mentoring Questions

Self-Leadership and Development

New demands are being made on leadership. We may be surprised to find that the world we all prepared for is not the world we will find ahead. In fact, the odds are we are in for many surprises. Numerous attempts have been made to describe our new era as the "post- industrial society," "information society," "computer age," or "internet age." So far we seem to be overusing these creative labels. The one clear message is: don't get left behind; don't become obsolete. I have to change as well. As a professional business leader, I need a strategy to increase the odds that I will successfully stay in the game. That is what the following material addresses.

Change, Competition, and Complexity

To be a leader in this environment begs the question: how must I be different to be an effective leader? The competitive edge tomorrow will belong to those who know how to inspire more productivity and excellence from each individual while building a high per-formance- team. This requires new knowledge and an understand-ing of how to use it. Business managers are beginning to realize that doing what they always have done will not produce the pre-ferred results. This means development for both individuals and teams. Given that all development is self-development, it is vital to understand the role and importance of self-leadership in this major cultural shift.

Change

We are in a new era, one of accelerating change. Change begets change. Change of all types—economic, social, cul-tural, technological, and political—is occurring at an increasing rate. While change is happening in so many areas of the business environment, we continue to see many busi-nesses unprepared to react. Too many businesses are being caught by surprise by what is happening in their market place. Small-to medium-sized businesses, managed by founders/owners, appear to be most vulnerable. Many are relying on business strategies and practices that have not been seriously updated in the past five years. Leaders so often have not been and are not currently involved in sys-tematic preparation to meet the future. Everything is chang-ing but the leaders.

Competition

Today's competition takes place on a global scale. Discussions with high-technology leaders indicate they never know from whence the next competitive attack will come: United States, Europe, India, China, or Japan. They just know it will come. They are in a race that is knowledge based, a race that is spreading throughout business. Non-technology based businesses are being affected as well, but often they are based on technological advances. Fueling international competition is the compelling drive around the world for people to improve their own standard of living. They (those seeking economic fulfillment) want to come to the same banquet table the people in the United States have been enjoying for decades. They too want to enjoy the goods and services of a material culture. They not only want to be in the game—they want to win it. The need for us all to reshape our thinking and skills is apparent.

Complexity
Another characteristic of the new era is the increasing complexity of almost everything we do. Consider the impact of the computer. To put this in perspective, think about the birthday card that when opened, plays the "Happy Birthday" tune. That represents where computer technology was about fifty years ago.

Now I not only have a desktop computer, but I also have a laptop and a handheld computer. I organize my business life as well as my personal life via computer. I make stock transactions; travel arrangements; restaurant reservations; as well as buy my favorite coffee, business books, and my wife's birthday present over the internet. And my ten-year-old grandson is light-years ahead of me in navigating the computer. So what is the bottom line? Each of us faces a choice: whether to stand idly by and become a victim or rise to the challenge of the new era.

Taking Responsibility
Unless we have a deliberate strategy to deal with change, change will deal with us. Preparedness not only requires a strategy for change but a changing strategy. While change is inevitable, its impact cannot be fully assessed before the fact. Therefore, the best approach is to create a strategy to cope with and prosper from change. Rather than a static strategy, such as one that is based on a given percentage increase in market share, it should be a dynamic strategy, focused on the delivery system—the people. The most potent strategy will focus on building the resource that will acquire

not only market share but, more importantly, create the business products and processes that drive the business success, measured by bottom-line results.

Creating a culture or atmosphere of anticipation in a business is one of the most effective means of dealing with change. Anticipation creates the best kind of preparedness, and, anticipation is a continuous process. Many businesses, like people, don't prepare to make a change until there is a crisis or a wake-up call. The answer is to develop a crisis-prevention strategy.

In other words, rather than coping with superimposed change, as others do, develop a preferred strategy that keeps you and your business in a state of anticipation. This kind of process develops focused thinking about what needs to be done next to stay healthy—unlike the average hapless business about to be sideswiped by change it hasn't seen coming. As a precaution, take a look at yourself and see if you are providing the right kind of leadership—for yourself and for your colleagues. Fundamentally, your success as a leader is impacted by your self-leadership.

Coming to grips with self-leadership is an important step in developing the ability to manage others. As a manager, you cannot help develop others unless you, too, are in the process of gaining knowledge and information. Personal development is the source from which you can guide and encourage others' growth and development.

Members of the senior management group must be the encouragers, models, and facilitators. If you are not modeling personal development and demonstrating its benefits, then it will be a tough sell to those whom you are responsible for leading.

More and more people in the business environment—particularly knowledge workers—will have to manage and lead themselves. You will have to focus your energies where they can make the greatest contribution; you will have to learn to develop yourself to meet the challenges you face. You will have to learn to stay vibrant and healthy throughout your working life. You will have to learn how and when to change what you do, how you do it, and when you do it.

The average working life for knowledge workers is fifty years, with people likely to keep working until they are around seventy-five years of age or older. But the life expectancy of the average business is only thirty years—and dropping. Increasingly, knowledge workers will outlive any one employer and will have to be prepared to move their job and possibly their career field. This phenomenon will increasingly place new demands on the knowledge worker to be in a constant growth mode.

Knowledge as a Resource

So what's the objective? In the beginning, it is to acquire beneficial knowledge for you and your organization. Facilitating a strategic learning program is a good starting point to prepare you and your colleagues to respond effectively to the changing environment. This is the classic win-win arrangement. With the mobility of careers from business-to-business, as well as the need to have practiced managers in key slots, management development is at the heart of a successful career and a successful business.

Management development is both the objective and, in part, the reward. While development and learning do not assure success, they certainly enhance the probability of achieving and sustaining it, as opposed to the alternative. Part of management's task is to help the culture embrace the concept that self-development/self-leadership is a powerful and rewarding process individually and corporately. The culture should support, even encourage, individuals to take responsibility for their own futures through self-leadership.

A Learning Organization

As a manager, it is your job to acquire knowledge on behalf of the organization so you can intelligently execute your responsibilities. The individual manager is in the best position to assess what knowledge is important for effective and successful performance on the job. An organization that encourages, supports, facilitates, and develops these qualities in its people can be called a learning organization or a learning company. A learning organization is a group of people who learn not only as individuals but also as a team. The process starts with a personal commitment. This is where character has a significant impact on the ability to execute a self-leadership process.

Winston Churchill once said, "The empires of the future are empires of the mind." As this thought takes root, consider the extent to which knowledge serves as the commodity that catapults successful companies into the future. All around us, we see successful organizations transforming themselves at a very rapid pace. In enlightened business environments, it has become well recognized that the way to increase the valuation of the business is to grow the intellectual capital through HR development.

For most of us, our work responsibilities and environment change constantly. Computer processing is replacing whole groups of workers who used to process paper. Part-time or contract workers are growing in number. Today, Manpower Inc., is the largest employer in the United States, providing temporary and contract workers to a vast spectrum of businesses. People employed as knowledge workers float from company to company, project to project. Job security is diminishing, particularly for those not keeping up with the knowledge explosion. Today, security comes from what you know how to do, what you can learn to do, and how well you can access knowledge through collaboration with others.

The ability to learn is becoming the new core competency. You will find that the greater your capacity for learning and building knowledge, the greater your chance to enjoy continuing success. This is true for both the individual and the enterprise. Tom Peters in his book, *Liberation Management,* put it quite succinctly: "Brains are in; heavy lifting out. Thence the development of knowledge is job one for corporations."

Learning is one of the three major development areas utilized by companies who are focused on growth. Along with learning, strategic growth targets include leadership and relationship skills. The expansion of one's leadership and relationship skills is grounded in expanded learning. The attainment of desired business goals requires a foundation in learning. Orchestrating learning is both challenging and rewarding. While it will come at a cost, the rewards are worth the investment.

Knowledge Management

As your business environment becomes increasingly complex, the easier it is to forget the things you should be doing. In the process of responding to constant demands on our time, it is too easy for the important issues to be displaced by the urgent. Unless a definite strategy for identification and progress is in place to review important issues, they will easily get pushed aside. This takes leadership.

An effective technique for dealing with this opportunity is to make it a regular part of a program for improvement and transformation—to revisit your core strategies on a regular basis. The mentoring culture supports this approach nicely, but it needs someone at the helm to make sure that the focus is on the key strategies and the business fundamentals.

Mentoring Continuous Learning

Management Focus

The fundamental responsibility of a senior management team is to run a profitable (an effective and a successful) business. This requires constant readiness. Business, in general, is not just evolving; it's exploding. Major business publications constantly provide readers with enormous amounts of information on changing markets. As business managers, what do we do to cope with all the uncertainty? Look to your people. Invest in them to meet the compounding challenges head-on.

Exceptional Financial Results

By all definitions, the main responsibility of the chief executivezis to produce the leadership and management discipline to achieve positive financial results. Without equivocation or doubt, that is number one. An executive can create all kinds of wonderful people programs and motivational strategies, but if they get in the way of achieving the preferred bottom line, problems will certainly develop.

The development of a learning organization should be supportive of developing the preferred financial results. In fact, a company without a commitment to develop its people, one that drives its human resources only for bottom-line results, may indeed do very well in the short term. Maintaining a balanced approach to achieving preferred bottom-line results must include building a renewal element into the engine of the business.

Renewal

Most senior managers have been using their human resources to achieve short-term results. Rarely is sufficient attention given to improving the delivery system, which is their people. Business pressures regularly result in managers looking after the urgent while neglecting the important. It's a familiar trap. However, if properly focused, a well-managed business can do both and achieve better results.

Several businesses I have dealt with or been a part of have had senior level managers espousing continuous learning. However, if the chief executive does not actively support such initiatives, they will lack the necessary impetus to become broadly embraced and practiced. Certainly, the chief executive has enough to look after. Yet, he or she really needs to be proactively involved in spreading the gospel, emphasizing the importance of the company's involvement in continuous learning and development—and he or she needs to model it. When the CEO models behavior, it becomes culture.

Competencies and Capabilities
As you consider the development of knowledge, it is helpful to consider its purpose and use. In that regard, determining whether you are striving for competency or capability is productive. Many people use the terms "competency" and "capability" interchangeably. This may lead to needless confusion. It is useful to differentiate these two distinct, yet critically interrelated aspects of organizational identity.

Core Knowledge Competencies
Authors C.K. Prahalad and Gary Hamel (*Competing for the Future*) suggest three tests of core knowledge competence:

1. It must make a disproportionate contribution to client- or customer-perceived value.
2. It must be competitively unique.
3. It forms the basis for entry into new service or product markets.

Usually companies seek to develop core competencies as a strategy for competitive advantage. The process often leads to an important redefining of the business. Rethinking the underlying values and assumptions, identifying new lines of business, and defining critical skill sets to support future needs is an extremely valuable process.

Core knowledge competencies are those domains of expertise, knowledge, and technical information that are unique to a particular type of business. They form the critical knowledge for the enterprise. Here are some examples of core knowledge competencies:

*   Technical knowledge of abrasives and adhesives (3M)
*   Pictorial imaging technology (Eastman Kodak)
*   Accounting practices (Arthur Andersen)
*   Extraction of petro-chemical products from crude oil (Chevron)
*   Development of software code (Microsoft)

- Gene splicing (Genetech)
- Color animation technologies (Disney)

Core Performance Capabilities

Core performance capabilities are functions and processes that enable an organization to deliver high-quality products and services with speed, efficiency, and high levels of customer satisfaction. These capabilities contribute significantly to the success of the enterprise. They form the critical behaviors for the enterprise. Here are a few examples of performance capabilities:

- Ability to bring new products to a market quickly (Hewlett-Packard)
- Capacity to quickly modify products and/or services (Rubber-maid)
- Sharing learning, insights, and best practices (Texas Instruments)
- Attracting and hiring quality employees (General Electric)
- Logistics management (Wal-Mart)
- Ability to reengineer core business processes (Nokia)
- Ability to continuously provide world-class customer service (Nordstrom)

Companies with exceptional performance capabilities usually have achieved their status through some highly focused process—it does not happen by chance. For example, anyone can have exceptional customer service, but the Nordstrom organization actually created the focus, commitment, and discipline to do it. This is not specifically knowledge based. This is persistent focus and performance.

On the other hand, look at the list of companies that have achieved prominence through their knowledge competencies. The people at Microsoft are in possession of unique and specific knowledge, which was required to achieve their prowess and success.

This is precisely what you must do to achieve—and maintain—high levels of success. While performance is extremely important, knowledge—the continual development of new knowledge—is a foundational requirement for continuing business success.

Application

" IT'S SINK OR SWIM HERE. WE WEED OUT THE WEAK ONES REAL FAST! "

GE's Jack Welch said it all with his comment to *Fortune* magazine, "We spend all our time on people. The day we screw up the people thing, this company is over." In my quest for documenting the best business practices of successful companies, attention to HR development ranks high in corporate priorities and strategies. The really successful companies have a knowledge strategy. They have identified the knowledge that will create a higher probability in achieving their business strategies. They are not taking chances on people being involved in their own knowledge/-rescue—they are guiding the knowledge development so there does not have to be a rescue.

Here is a process I highly recommend in developing the critical business knowledge to create championship performance:

Three Key Steps to Develop Critical Business Knowledge

1. Appoint a knowledge development task force with the special purpose of identifying knowledge development needs. First actions should include the following steps:
    *   Develop an understanding of the importance of having the right knowledge in place as the starting point for building performance.
    *   Identify the core competencies of the business.
    *   Evaluate the current knowledge base—a general assessment of knowledge about the best business practices, particularly at the upper level of management.

2. Evaluate the company's strategic plan/business plan to ascertain the knowledge requirements for effective accomplishment.
    *   Do the knowledge capabilities exist for functional specialties?
    *   Have managers really been trained as managers? Are they developing their subordinates or are they still immersed in operations themselves?
    *   Have knowledge requirements been identified to help develop new products and services?

3. Draft a knowledge development strategy based on the results of the above activities. Present to corporate decision makers.

Essentially this is what my firm does for companies wanting to prepare their business for the future. We don't do all of these tasks ourselves; we facilitate the client under the direction of the CEO. Our role always is to help build the CEO's position as the leader of growth and development. He or she should set the pace and be the leader. Nothing communicates the importance of continuous

learning and development than having the CEO as the lead instiga-
tor and supporter of learning. I highly recommend Noel Tichy's
book, *The Leadership Engine—How Winning Companies Build
Leaders at Every Level,* for great insights into the effectiveness of
the CEO being the lead knowledge developer/teacher.

This increased involvement of the CEO in the learning process may
seem daunting to a CEO already working eighty hours. You are
probably wondering, "How do I fit it in?" A lot of CEOs are still
using old business models to run their business. They are in a comfort rut even though they are working an incredible number of
hours. They usually remain in that rut until they discover their
model is no longer doing the job. That realization usually is delivered along with some less-than-stellar business results. Then they
start to evaluate what they need to do differently.

I'm sure you realize the way to maintain a winning season is to
make sure your wins continue. Once the losses start, turn-around,
which is much harder, follows. The key strategy is preparation,
preparation, and preparation. How serious are you about producing
championship business performance? Yes, it takes leadership. Ask
yourself, and possibly an unbiased outsider, "What should I be
doing differently to get the results I want?"

The message I am delivering to more and more CEOs is that business is not for amateurs- not if you are looking at any long-term
opportunities. I'm currently working with a CEO who realized he
needed to make sure his team was prepared to get him to the next
level. He wants to grow his revenues by 50% in the next two years.
He is working in an industry and a business sector that it is entire-
ly possible for him to achieve his goal. All he has to do is execute.
He realizes this and asked me to help get his team ready. We have
completed the executive team assessment and are now developing
the training curriculum specifically designed to get his team playing at the highest possible level just as soon as it can.

His team is a bit varied with members' backgrounds that range from
as few as two years experience to one with over 17 years on the

executive staff. Also their educational backgrounds range from no college to a master's degree. They are very well versed in their industry knowledge, possibly the leaders in their sector. Like many executive teams/groups I encounter, they have not developed a whole company outlook. Here's where they usually are:

1. Operations Mindset—Most executives come up the ranks through a certain discipline, such as sales, marketing, or operations. That's the area where they have worked for most of their careers and most likely get compensated for how they perform in that area. They usually have a silo perspective, looking after their function, not the whole company. They need to think "company" when they sit with the executive team.

2. Strategic Perspective Generally Lacking—They have not been involved in any training that would prepare them to contribute at a very high level in strategic corporate business development. They need to understand and contribute to corporate strategic thinking. Thinking about a department and thinking about a company are very different.

3. Weak in Best Business Practices—Most individuals do not have a good understanding of the business basics or what I call the best business practices. The benefits of a meaningful review of the basics are (a) they need the knowledge to understand what is needed to produce positive business results (what successful companies do) and (b) learning together enables them to hold each other accountable—they all have the general knowledge of what to do; now they need the discipline to do it. Team learning helps develop this discipline.

4. Usually Lack Team Discipline—Most executive staffs have not learned what it means to work and function as a team. The term "team" is one of the most misunderstood and abused terms in the management lexicon. The executive staff and the company benefit greatly by learning

together—the disciplines, behaviors, and conventions of a great management team.

After I completed the executive assessment, I met with the CEO and presented mentoring curriculum that I proposed he and I facilitate. My objectives were to first support and enhance the CEO in his role of team leader. I coached him on how to be the chief knowledge officer for his team and his company. One of my goals was to prepare the CEO to be the knowledge leader. My presence as a facilitator in the process should not eclipse his leadership and his role. I wanted the focus to be on him, not me. I was there as his assistant.

The CEO is the head of an organization comprised primarily of knowledge workers. It's his or her responsibility to lead the process for his or her company of knowledge workers. The general of the army is responsible for making sure his or her soldiers are prepared for battle, know the battle plan and can execute; the football coach is responsible for his team's preparedness, including knowing how to play their positions and the game plan. Execution can be no better than the preparation, unless you are lucky—and you cannot go to the business Super Bowl counting on luck. The better you execute, the better the results. And the CEO is the person to lead the way.

Steve, the CEO, and I reviewed the training options and developed this plan. I would meet with him once a month for a four hour-session that would precede a four-hour session with his team. He and I would cover an agenda that he would prepare containing any issues he wished to discuss about the business, his mentoring of his staff, and the material we would be discussing with the team after our meeting.

Following are the critical knowledge summaries we use to get participants ready for a workshop. In that workshop we review (a) why this particular knowledge is important to the business, (b) what it looks like when deployed, and (c) how to put it to work immediately. Steve and I agreed on six workshops over a six-month period. He is well on his way to becoming a keen chief knowledge officer.

Critical Knowledge Summaries
(Just-in-time Business Intelligence)

1. Vision, Strategic Planning, and Implementation—This assures that executive managers are clear on the direction of the business and what steps are required to execute well.

2. The Corporate Performance Scorecard—Focusing on the best business metrics to achieve the preferred business results is key to success. All the players need to know the score.

3. Financial Management—Introduction to the essential elements of a comprehensive financial management process. This gets the whole executive team on the same financial page.

4. The Practice of Management—A basic review of what managers need to know and do to function effectively. Too few managers know this.

5. Driving Value through Activity-Based Management—Knowing each activity's contribution to profit and what can be done to improve the process are an essential ingredients for continued success in a competitive marketplace.

6. Building a Performance Culture—The business culture shapes workers' attitudes. Knowing how to create a high-performance culture can unleash exceptional performance.

7. Quality As an Essential Strategy—Only excellence earns a profit. Quality in all aspects of the business operations is part of successful companies' business strategy.

8. Creating Championship Teams—Most executives work in groups—not teams. This material addresses how to achieve exceptional business results through team collaboration and execution.

9. Relationship Skills—Using Your Emotional Intelligence—Relationships create the conduit through which championship performance flows. Relationship skills are becoming the most valuable skills in high-performance cultures.

10. Developing Leadership at All Levels—This covers the power of dispersed, motivated "workleaders": workers who lead and leaders who work, a must in today's flat organizations.

11. Self-Leadership—Taking Responsibility—Any change process starts with the individual. This involves a close look at how to increase personal effectiveness.

12. Creating A Learning Organization—In the age of the knowledge worker, you need to consider how to keep your most valuable resource, your people, involved in continuous learning.

My experience in similar engagements is that the team grows at a fast pace and enjoys the process. Here are the benefits of this approach:

1. The CEO is developing his or her leadership role as team leader.
2. The team is learning business basics that they will apply individually and corporately.
3. The team learns how to work together.
4. Each participant learns how to mentor his or her subordinates.

As the team members go through the learning process together, three powerful and interesting results occur. First, the team members acquire critical, needed business knowledge. Second, since they all know the business basics now, they hold each other accountable. And third, they understand what effective business teams do, together, to create great results. It's a powerful process.

Mentoring Questions

Here are a few specific topics around which to develop mentoring sessions. Let the leaders show the way.

1. Business Knowledge Needs
   - How do you know whether or not your business is missing out on greater success due to unconscious incompetence?
   - Could some bit of knowledge really make a difference in your business results?
   - Do you know the core knowledge that your business depends on? How are you growing it?

2. Knowledge to Be an Effective Manager
   - Are your managers prepared to get the most from your knowledge workers?
   - How much preparation and training are they getting?
   - Do you see any parallel with a winning—or losing – sports team?
   - Are all of your managers in the game to win?
   - What if some knowledge you don't have right now would help your managers increase your bottom line by 50%?

3. Core Knowledge Competencies
   - Have you identified the knowledge areas that your business depends on for your business results?
   - How competent are your colleagues?
   - How much are you leaving to chance?
   - What is your current strategy to build your core knowledge competencies?
   - How is it working?

4. Effective Leadership Traits
   - How are your management team members as leaders?
   - Do they know the traits of leaders and are they working to develop them?

- How much is leadership encouraged?
- Is your business culture supportive of leadership development?

5. Personal Mastery
   - If all development is self-development, how do you get people motivated to develop?
   - Should there be incentives for self-development?
   - Who benefits?
   - What do you think of a personal growth plan?
   - How much should the company be involved in a personal growth plan?

6. Knowledge of Technology Trends Affecting Business
   - Is someone in your organization tracking technology to understand any future opportunities or threats?
   - Is someone looking for technology that would make your business more productive or profitable?
   - What knowledge areas should you be developing for the good of the business?

7. Sharing Knowledge
   - Do some people in your organization believe that not sharing knowledge makes their job more secure?
   - How do you counteract that attitude?
   - Is the culture such that it rewards/encourages knowledge sharing?
   - What benefits are there in sharing knowledge?
   - Isn't collaboration a form of knowledge sharing?

8. Commitment to Continuous Learning
   - Why do you think so many businesses in the small-to-medium sector do not have continuous learning initiatives?
   - What's wrong with cutting HR development funds when a business encounters a budget crunch?

For Further Reading—Mentoring Material

Verna Allee, *The Knowledge Evolution: Expanding Organizational Intelligence* (New York: Butterworth-Heinemann, 1997).

Noel Tichey, *The Leadership Engine—How Winning Companies Build Leaders at Every Level* (New York: HarperBusiness, 1997).

Peter M. Senge, *The Fifth Discipline* (New York: Doubleday, 1990).

Daniel R. Tobin, *Transformational Learning: Renewing Your Company Through Knowledge and Skills* (New York: John Wiley & Sons, 1996).

Peter B. Vaill, *Learning as a Way of Being* (San Francisco: Jossey-Bass, 1996).

Chapter 14
Institutionalizing Mentoring

"All leaders, no matter how charismatic or visionary, eventually die. but a visionary company does not necessarily die, not if it has the organizational strngth to transcend any individual leader and remain visionary and vibrant decade after decade and through multiple generations."
—James C. Collins & Jerry I. Porras
"Built to Last"

- Continuous Learning
- The CEO as Leader-Mentor
- The Mentoring Hierarchy
- Mentoring Greatness Through Leader-Mentors
- Preparation, Preparation, Preparation
- The Leader-Mentor Gameplan

Continuous Learning

Effective managers focus on how they can make those above them, as well as those below them, as successful as possible. In a knowledge-based business environment, that involves continuous knowledge creation and application. Individually, continuous learning and development will be most effective when aligned with career objectives. Random learning may be worthwhile, but it is not as useful as learning that is targeted at a specific goal. Goal-oriented learning requires a clear understanding of career direction, business opportunities, and development needs.

I have seen many judgment errors made in promoting individuals into positions for which they were not quite prepared. This is one of the most pervasive problems in business management. Companies are still promoting the best salespeople, computer specialists, engineers, accountants, and marketing specialists into management positions without providing adequate training and development. A lot of them make the transition. But quite a few don't, and the result usually is the loss of a good pre-management contributor and the creation of an under-performing department. This is very expensive turnover. We not only lose the good worker but the momentum during the unsuccessful management transition. While this is difficult to measure, it nevertheless is significant.

A careful screening for realistic career objectives, supported by management-facilitated development, can be a proactive solution to future management needs. Companies that enjoy prolonged business success have as one of their major contributors a joint career development program with their employees. A strategic mentoring program can be such a catalyst.

Individual Growth Potential

You can get into more trouble by not knowing your limitations than by knowing only your strengths. You can respond positively when you know your limitations. Then you can factor in your compensating strategy. Developing an understanding of limitations is a focused exercise that should take place at the outset of any development process.

Specific Growth Targets

A comprehensive plan with specific growth targets will assist in realizing the greatest growth benefit for both the individual and the organization. Both individuals and businesses need to develop in ways that will support the realization of long-term success. Management benefits by recognizing the common goal and supporting it. The individual benefits by increasing his or her abilities and value to the business.

A comprehensive human-resource development plan for the organization is an important piece of work to guide this strategic process. Regrettably, not very many of these development plans are produced and implemented so that they capitalize on the enormously positive results such plans can produce. This is a huge opportunity for any business but particularly the small- to medium-sized business emerging from entrepreneurial leadership.

Achieving Career Goals

Only infrequently do people actually achieve what they long for in their careers. But when they do achieve their objectives, it is usually the result of a series of thoughtful choices. For most people, however, circumstances rather than choices determine the courses of their careers. On the other hand, I've noticed that people who have achieved fulfillment in their careers are those who are in control of themselves, their careers, their relationships, and the conditions around them.

Control in this case is not some heavy-handed or clandestine, manipulative process. Rather, being in control means having an awareness of choices and being proactive in its pursuit. The importance of realizing the need to make choices rather than acquiescing to circumstances should be noted. Identifying what you really want is foundational to the process.

Sustained Commitment to Leadership Development

Leadership development programs remain meaningful only so long as the CEO and senior executives remain personally committed to their existence. Unless the senior management team is fully committed and deeply involved in the development process, its value definitely will be diminished and, unfortunately, the results that could energize and transform the business will not be realized.

The first step is to make sure the company makes a sustainable commitment, which will produce a process with ongoing value. All too often, initiatives such as leadership development begin with all the goodwill and enthusiasm an organization can possibly muster. But soon the novelty wears off, the drudgery begins, commitment slackens, and what was an enthusiastic beginning becomes merely a mediocre process.

Self-leadership is an essential ingredient to the successful business. A cadre of management leaders committed to be prepared to play the game at the highest level of their abilities is what creates sustained success. It's a noble objective.

"YOUR REPORT MAKES IT CLEAR, BRICKFORD, YOU HAVEN'T BECOME ACQUAINTED WITH THE TERM 'KNOWLEDGE WORKER'."

The CEO as Leader-Mentor

Any major impact in cultural change in the enterprise must come from the top. And the kind of change you are working to achieve with a company-wide commitment for mentoring will be as successful as the CEO wishes to make it. It's up to you—the CEO. Pockets of greatness can be created by an enterprising manager. And the importance of making beachheads of improvement should not be diminished. Many fine examples of CEOs being challenged to support beneficial business initiatives after seeing the benefits modeled by rising stars in their organization are evident. But it's usually faster and ultimately more effective if the CEO can be the primary sponsor.

One of my CEO friends who has really impressed me regularly looks for challenging business material to bring to his executive staff. Here is the process he takes his team through. He asks his team members to read the material and reflect on it with the admonition to look for application to their business. When they meet he reviews these questions with them:

Business Improvement Starters

1. What does this material mean to you as a senior business leader?

2. What does it mean to your colleagues on your management team?

3. What does it mean for the company?

4. What actions are implied for:
   - You?
   - The management team?
   - Your company?

5. Does it identify any opportunities for you?

6. What changes should you consider in your goals, strategies, policies or structures?

7. If you knew this before, why haven't you acted on it?

8. What specific actions should you take now? Why?

What does this kind of approach suggest to you? To me, it is the perfect manifestation of the attitude "What else can we or should we be doing to create the best results?" Success is not a destination—it is one long, bumpy, difficult, continuous trip. You need to be making corrections regularly to make sure you are still on course. And those corrections need to be timely, well thought-out and well executed. Don't forget the essence of leadership is performance. Leadership of knowledge workers must involve continuous learning and application of that knowledge, and how to put it to work now.

The Mentoring Hierarchy

I introduced the mentoring hierarchy in chapter 5 ("The Manager Mentoring Process/Hierarchy"). Please review that process again in view of the material covered in the subsequent chapters in terms of the knowledge content that can be introduced throughout the organization. Do you see the enormous opportunities to create knowledge that will make a difference in your organization?

One interesting point about knowledge workers I have found is they are open to learning and continuing to add to the intellectual capital base of the business. Smart leadership can see this opportunity and feed the process, actually systematize it, assuring a goal, a process, and a review-mechanism exist to assure the process is achieving the desired ends. However, as pointed out in the material on systematic management (chapter 10), a system must have a champion to flourish or even survive.

Mentoring Greatness Through Leader-Mentors

The key thought I hope that has made an impression is the potential of a broad-based mentoring program in creating a great future, even greatness. Imagine a company full of mentor-leaders keeping the corporate business intellect growing. In that context, I have been involved with two kinds of mentoring.

The first I would call *reactive-remedial*—This happens when business leaders realize they now have a problem and need to respond.

They suddenly realize they are facing a situation for which they need counsel, guidance, or some kind of sounding board. Sometimes business leaders just call for help. They realized something was wrong and, at the moment, the solution exceeded their resources. This often opens the door later to the second type I am about to describe.

The second type I call *proactive-constructive*. Here you can have the initiative. You can implement strategic action to create powerful results. If you really desire greatness, and are motivated, to improve your company's performance, then exercise the leadership to build the kind of knowledge—then practices—that produce exceptional performance. This is where the payoff is.

I am compelled to call attention to the way professional sports teams build greatness—they call them dynasties when they create a good run (something like GE). Consider for a moment the process:

Steps to Build a Great Company

- Recruit the best available players.
- Mentor/coach the rookies so they can become starters.
- Make sure everyone knows the plays and the gameplan.
- Make each individual responsible to keep in condition and contribute.
- Understand the importance of teamwork and supporting your fellow player.
- Be diligent and alert in looking for improvement opportunities.
- Scout the competition and know what you have to do better.
- Play by the rules, but do everything you can to win the game.

Who wins in the game of business? Sure, the lucky win once in a while, but what's the predictability of that happening? I don't leaving my business success to chance. And neither do any of the smart business leaders I know. To the contrary, they are looking for the edge, the way to get ahead of the curve. In today's business environment, that takes leadership with absolute resolve. Are you the kind of leader that can lead your business to championship results? If your answer is affirmative, then be prepared to increase your focus and resolve—that's what it will take.

The realization that the era of the knowledge worker has arrived has not been reflected in the behaviors of a lot of the businesses in the sector my firm serves—small-to mid-size businesses. I know performance can be improved immensely through a well-conceived and executed mentoring plan. All it takes is leadership.

I spoke at a conference recently and spent some time with a remarkable CEO who is one of the more impressive examples of what great leadership can accomplish. His name is Boyd Baugh and he is chairman of Pivot Interiors, Inc., one of the world's largest Herman Miller dealers. Boyd had a spot on the program to share his story about growing his remarkable company using open-book management. Boyd has four partners who joined him in the process of building a great company. One of his partners, Barbara Carlyle, who also spoke, related how she had merged her company, another Herman Miller dealer, with Boyd's. One of the first steps she took was to engage an industrial psychologist to interview them and determine if their values meshed. How discerning. They were thrilled with the results when it was revealed they all had very similar values—ones that have proven they can work well together and create loyalty and commitment in their company.

After spending two days with these people at the conference, I could see great relationships in action among the partners. Also, I observed that Boyd had the characteristics of many of the great business leaders I have had the privilege to know. I was attracted to his style and wanted to learn more about his leadership and his company. I had just read Jim Collins's new book, *Good to Great,* and Boyd was looking like a "Level 5" leader (see chapter 11) that Collins describes.

I now know he is. Boyd invited me to visit him at his company and attend an employee "performance huddle."

Boyd shared with me that his company practices open-book management where senior management shares the company's financial information with all the employees. He believes that if you want your colleagues to act like owners, then you have to treat them like owners. True to his convictions, his company has had an employee stock ownership plan for over eleven years. The "performance huddle" was powerful. It has evolved into a very meaningful weekly meeting that focuses on performance—reported by the manager who has the responsibility for that performance and its impact on the company's financial results.

Each manager reports on his or her specific line item in the company financial report, which is projected on a screen for everyone to see. The data is live, with the CFO entering the numbers as each manager reports them. Weekly they report their numbers which produces an instant, updated look at how the company is performing—instant accountability! It was fascinating to observe the interest level—there were eighty to ninety people present—as each number was reported and the overall results were taking form.

Boyd later mentioned that they had participated in a program identified in the book by Jack Stack, *The Great Game of Business*. Stack developed some remarkable open-book practices developed at his company, SRC. The Pivot Interiors management team incorporated many of these practices into their own processes, producing a very committed work force. After the huddle, I asked Boyd if I could ask him some questions about his background, leadership style, and philosophy. Here's Boyd's leadership profile:

- *Background*—Boyd's first job out of college was in personnel. He learned the process and importance of hiring good people. His company went from 100 people to 7,000 in about five years while responsible for the personnel department. He eventually left that position to take on a new experience—selling school furniture. He became the top salesperson in the company his first year by focusing on an innovative approach of identifying what the needs of the customer were and how to best meet them. Boyd mentioned this was a unique approach at the time. He has always been interested in innovation so he applied it to designing innovative classrooms and hit a home run. This led him into innovative office interiors with Herman Miller in 1976.

- *Values*—Core values of honesty, integrity, and treating others with dignity and respect have guided his business experiences. All of his employees must adhere to this code or they cannot be in the company. There is no tolerance on the value issue.

- *Knowledge Development*—He has been blessed with an intellectual curiosity regarding finding a more innovative approach to whatever the task. "What if we tried to..." always seemed like a good place to start when tackling a problem. He had several mentors along the way, but one of the first always challenged him for a more innovative approach to any problem. Boyd has always been a reader and taken courses. Also, he has been very active in industry organizations; currently he is chairman of the Office Furniture Dealers Association. In line with his innovative bent, he started a study group of office furniture dealers to meet and evaluate best practices. They constantly pursued innovation—new and better ways to build their businesses by doing a better job of understanding their customers' needs. Boyd has provided regular training in his company, being a believer in constantly learning something new.

- *Management/Leadership Philosophy*—I then asked Boyd to provide an overview of his management and leadership philosophy. Here are the highlights.

  - <u>*Shared Ownership*</u>—This has been a great way to attract and keep the best people.

- *Open-book management*—An effective way to communicate that everyone has a stake in what is happening, supporting the ownership culture.
- *Accountability*—Part of the ownership culture is to be responsible and accountable.
- *Hire the best*—Never settle for mediocrity. If you want a first-class business, you have to hire first-class people—and keep them.
- *Training*—You cannot hire the best people and not give them the best tools. Training and the right systems and equipment keep them at the peak of effectiveness. That's where you want to focus in order to be innovative in meeting your customers' needs.

Toward the end of our meeting, I asked what specifically Boyd could recommend as a guide to building and sustaining a great company. His response: "Keep true to your values and stay the course." That is what Boyd has done, and he has a great company. Yes, this approach really works.

Preparation, Preparation, Preparation

So how do you get your team ready to play at the highest level? You need to mentor and coach the kind of behaviors that will produce the best business results. This is the area of business performance that has the greatest opportunity for major improvement. First, consider the process of employee appraisals. Have you ever seen a really well-executed process? Not many exist. It is not easy to sit across the table from a colleague and give feedback. It is one of the more difficult areas to administer for both managers and the HR department. Managers avoid it and usually have to be pressured to finally get the appraisal job done. And, the process seldom achieves the positive results sought. Most organizations have not come up with a process that is supported by those who have to use it. The process is viewed as a necessary evil rather than an opportunity.

Here is an opportunity to achieve major benefits in building corporate performance by joining the appraisal process with the mentoring process. Use mentoring targets for appraisal purposes. Here's how it would work:

1. Identify precisely what it is you want the person playing the particular position to achieve.
2. Train, mentor, and coach to produce high-level performance.
3. Put responsibility on each player to rate himself or herself in agreed performance areas.
4. Tie in with incentives.
5. Complete the appraisal process.

Numerous variations on this theme exist. I have seen exceptional results achieved through this process. Following is an example of such an appraisal process. I'm sure you can find ways to improve on it for your specific needs.

Mentor-Leader Appraisal Criteria

Rank on a scale of 1 to 10.

1-2	Weaknesses are putting the company at risk -needs immediate attention
3-4	Underachieving/vulnerable
5-6	Maintaining performance—doing the job
7-8	Good—creating the right direction for the right results
9-10	Excellent, forward-looking, preparing the business for the future

1. Strategic Planning and Implementation
   a. Has visibility on significant work to be accomplished while systematically executing business strategies
   b. Employs meaningful metrics to manage and communicate performance
   c. Achieves work systematically—uses planning in place of firefighting
   d. Anticipates and prepares to achieve the preferred results
   e. Manages work of subordinates to achieve work on a timely basis

2. Financial Management
   a. Knows the numbers that make a difference in financial performance
   b. Uses financial information to target performance initiatives
   c. Develops understanding of those around him or her of significance of the numbers

    d.   Has financial targets and effectively organizes to achieve them

    e.   Subordinates are numbers conscious and are contributing to improvement initiatives

3. Systematic Management
    a.   Understands responsibilities of a manager and models effectively
    b.   Effectively manages the systems and processes under his or her management
    c.   Has documentation and visibility of each system/process
    d.   Subordinates involved in developing system/process improvement initiatives
    e.   Achieves high level of predictability of positive results

4. Leadership
    a.   Identifies improvement opportunities and takes responsibility for results
    b.   Effective in communication and developing productive followership
    c.   Develops trust and models values to build strong corporate culture
    d.   Develops understanding and support for corporate objectives
    e.   Effective in developing subordinates

5. Relationships
    a.   Understands and models high-performance relationships
    b.   Builds relationship skills in subordinates
    c.   Builds enthusiastic and positive attitudes for work accomplishment
    d.   Is sought out as a counselor/mentor
    e.   Develops positive customer reaction, inside and outside the organization

6. Learning & Growth
    a.   An enthusiastic learner—consistently seeking new, usable knowledge
    b.   Has mastered core knowledge competencies for your industry
    c.   Shares knowledge and encourages others to do so
    d.   Motivates and leads subordinates in learning and growth
    e.   Anticipates knowledge needs personally and corporately

---

Using this model, you can develop the specific behaviors you need to produce championship business performance—and reward your players accordingly. Various reward levels can be designed from the accumulated points—and you can weight those that have the greatest need to be achieved.

Here is a good example. Recently I was sitting with the board of directors of a client company. We were engaged to assist in developing a business perpetuation strategy. A particular manufacturing division was under review that day, including the most effective incentives for the new general manager (G.M.). For his first six months the new G.M. had been tasked to concentrate on the bottom line. At the end of the six months, after reviewing his performance and at the recommendation of the CEO, the board took two astute actions. The new G.M. had impressed the board with his results, including having identified a significant inventory surplus that could be converted to cash. The board awarded a performance bonus on the first six months performance, which was bottom-line oriented, The bonus incentive for the next period was changed to converting inventory surplus to cash, which would create a negative result on the bottom line yet produce much needed cash. Is the new G.M. motivated? Absolutely.

Leader-Mentor Gameplan

So what do you have to do to field a championship business team? First of all, you have to be totally committed—you must have absolute resolve. This calls for committed, focused leadership. Put together your gameplan and try it out on your colleagues. Keep in mind where their thinking is in this process. Are they in the same game, league, or sport? Don't blindside them with your unbridled enthusiasm until you have at a minimum prepared them for some level of appreciation of what you want to accomplish. Here are five key steps to consider in developing your gameplan.

Five Key Steps to Mentoring Greatness

1. <u>Consider the Keys and Processes For Making Change Happen (presented in chapter 6).</u>
Make sure you have evaluated what it takes to successfully orchestrate change that will affect most of your business operations.

2. <u>Determine who the champion is going to be.</u>

The CEO is in the right position to provide lasting influence and guidance.

3. <u>Train every manager as a mentor.</u>
Provide each manager with the training to truly mentor the kind of performance that will stimulate championship performance throughout the organization.

4. <u>Provide incentives for successful mentoring.</u>
Create incentives for your colleagues to help you build the value of the business. Incorporate the mentoring function into the regular performance evaluation.

5. <u>Construct mentoring incentives around the mentoring of the six disciplines of exceptional performance.</u>
Mentoring the knowledge that will improve business performance is the place to start.

As a leader of your business, your objective is to institutionalize the behaviors that will build and perpetuate great performance. Everyone wants to be on the winning team. Don't let your teammates down. Show them the way to greatness. Help create the impetus for a business committed to greatness and ready to win the big game. There are no losers, only winners.

For Further Reading—Mentoring Material

Phillip C. McGraw, *Life Strategies—Doing What Works, Doing What Matters* (New York: Hyperion, 1999).

Tom DeMarco, *Slack: Getting Past Burnout, Busywork, and the Myth of Total Efficiency* (New York: Broadway Books, 2001).

Denis Waitley, *Empires of the Mind* (New York: William Morrow, 1995).

Epilogue

You have no doubt noted I have passion for the growth and application of knowledge. It's not only a great process for business, it's a life-extending exercise. Look how long great learners and educators have lived. They have kept the main muscle for life—the brain—active and in shape. Look at our national business treasure Peter Drucker, actively consulting and writing in his nineties. I believe continuous learning is a great prescription for longevity for both the individual and business. History bears this out. May you be blessed with long-term greatness.

Hal Johnson

About the Author

After graduating from the University of Southern California in 1961 with a bachelor's degree in social science, Hal Johnson began his career with the City of Los Angeles budget office. There he spent nine years developing his management abilities through increasingly responsible assignments. During this period, he received a full-tuition scholarship that enabled him to earn a master's degree in Public Administration.

In 1971, he became the first director of management services for the city of Portland in the newly centralized finance and administration office. Four years later, he moved to the private sector and began focusing on transitioning companies into management cultures based on shared management and leadership principles, emphasizing high performance.

For the subsequent twenty-plus years, Hal served as CEO in eight different companies, generally transitioning organizations from entrepreneurial to team-management cultures, with special emphasis on work measurement, personnel development, and performance. Most recently, he served as CEO of Transax PLC, based in Birmingham, England, Europe's largest check guarantee company followed by PolyVue Technologies Inc., a vision industry technology company in Marin County, California.

In the course of becoming a business-transition specialist, he has developed a unique and effective mentoring strategy that enables companies to develop their human resources to achieve exceptional performance.

In addition to serving on several boards of directors, Hal is chairman and CEO of LeadershipONE, Inc. He serves as a consultant, writer, and lecturer, both domestically and internationally. He resides with his wife, Adeline, in Larkspur, California, just north of San Francisco. They are the parents of a married son, Brad (wife-Joy); a married daughter, Michelle (husband-Kevin); and have two brilliant grandchildren, Rachel and Kyle.

Mentoring Resources

LeadershipONE, Inc., is a leader in the field of leadership assessment and executive development. Our mission is to provide knowledge, tools, and advisory services to evolving companies focused on helping prepare senior management to achieve exceptional business performance in a hyper-change environment. Successful implementation of our proprietary methodology can enable management to build an exceptional company that is future prepared More change will occur in the next ten years than occurred in the past fifty. Few companies are prepared and many won't survive. The key to being successful is based on a strategy of preparedness. Preparedness resides in assisting the company's leadership to achieve competence using best management practices. It all starts with the executive leadership, and we can show you how to prepare your company for championship performance.

Other resources available by the author:

MENTORING for Exceptional Performance (Glendale: Griffin Publishing Group, 1997).

Critical Knowledge Summary—Strategic Planning and Implementation (Anaheim: Sunnyhill Publishing, 2001).

Critical Knowledge Summary—Strategic Financial Performance (Anaheim: Sunnyhill Publishing, 2001).

Critical Knowledge Summary—The Systematic Practice of Management (Anaheim: Sunnyhill Publishing, 2001).

Critical Knowledge Summary—Developing Leadership—

At All Levels (Anaheim: Sunnyhill Publishing, 2001).

Critical Knowledge Summary—Developing Relationship Skills (Anaheim: Sunnyhill Publishing, 2001).

Critical Knowledge Summary—Mentoring Learning and Growth (Anaheim: Sunnyhill Publishing, 2000).

Contact information:

info@leadershipone.net
www.leadershipone.net

San Francisco, Sacramento, Los Angeles, Seattle